Caring Enough to Help

Counseling at a Crisis Pregnancy Center

Ellen Curro

BAKER BOOK HOUSE
Grand Rapids, Michigan 49516

ISBN: 0–8010–2551–6

Printed in the United States of America

To
the committed volunteers,
board members,
and friends
of Shady Grove Pregnancy Center
whose lives of love and courage
have forever changed my life.

Contents

Part Four
On a Mission

Acknowledgments

To those who have believed in me over the years that I could even consider attempting a book.

To Judie Brown, President of American Life League, who provided the opportunity to write and publish six of these letters that motivated me to write more.

To the volunteers who shared their struggles and joys as they loved the women and men who walked through the doors of the Pregnancy Center.

To Catherine Doherty and the Madonna House staff who continued to provide inspiration.

Thanks to my parents, family, and friends who encouraged me to keep writing.

Thanks to the board and intercessors of Linking Education and Medicine, Inc., who stood by me when family crisis hit during the middle of this process.

Special thanks to Siggie Ogan for typing and retyping the manuscript with enthusiasm.

To my Father in heaven, may you be praised forever!

Introduction

Do you like to eavesdrop? Pretend you're on a jet headed cross-country, and you overhear the following conversation between the two people seated behind you.

Jack: "Hi! My name is Jack Davis."

Ellen: "And my name is Ellen Curro."

J: "I'm a lawyer—a judge, actually. What do you do?"

E: "I work at a pregnancy center."

J: "You work at a what?"

E: "A pregnancy center."

J: "Is that a buzz-word?"

E: "No, I'm director of a pregnancy center."

J: "Do you get people pregnant, or unpregnant, or what?"

E: "We offer a free pregnancy test to see if they are pregnant and then help them look at their choices. . . ."

That was the start of a four-and-a-half-hour conversation that proved delightful, engaging, and a real "box-blower" for both of us. Jack blew my box of a "judge" (he was dressed in jeans, a chambray shirt, and a bolo tie). And I blew his box of a "pro-lifer." In fact, Jack, a pro-abortion judge in the court system, didn't figure out I was a pro-lifer until three-and-a-half hours into the discussion. That happened after hours of significant sharing from both of us, when I reached into my purse for a tissue and accidentally pulled out "Precious Preborn" (a model of a ten-to-twelve-week-old preborn child). Jack had seen those models in a courtroom, and his immediate association was "crazy, radical pro-lifer."

The abortion issue does polarize people. It is probably the most volatile moral issue of our day. Both camps, pro-abortion and pro-life, are guilty of putting others into boxes—stereotyping the other side.

That plane-ride conversation allowed me to see this issue through Jack's eyes as a judge, and I gave him a peek into my life at a crisis pregnancy center. Our lives were changed that day. We will never be the same. We opened ourselves to growing in knowledge, understanding, compassion, and friendship.

Whatever your position on abortion—I invite you to journey with me, to experience the lives of the women (and men) who are caught in the life-or-death choice. Meet the heroes who freely give of their valuable time, energy, and talents to reach out to women in crisis. Feel the intensity of emotions surrounding the abortion/pro-life debate from a grassroots level.

Each chapter is titled "Dear Sis." As you read letters to my sister know that I am writing to you, my sisters and brothers everywhere. Macrina Wiederkehr, in *A Tree Full of Angels* (New York: Harper & Row, 1988, p. 105) states:

> Letters are the stories of our souls. Unlike a telephone call, a letter can be picked up again and again. It can be deeply pondered. It can be eaten. Always serve letters with a cup of tea and a footstool. Celebrate "the reading" slowly. It is irreverent to read a letter fast.

There are thirty-one letters, one for each day of the month. Taste the tensions, joys, heartaches, and frustrations. Savor the insights that spur you to new growth. Ponder the humanness of those you will meet in crisis pregnancy centers. Celebrate God's intervention in the lives of ordinary people.

Come, take a peek into the heart of a crisis pregnancy center. . . .

PART **One**
(Extra) Ordinary Days

1

I Can See

Dear Sis,

I often wonder, Why am I in this work? But on days like today I know the answer. Let me share what happened.

My work as director of a crisis pregnancy center is intense, rewarding, and at times consuming. Ours is a Christian center where our dependence on God is recognized every day. We have many people outside the clinic praying for us, in addition to the volunteers and paid staff, who gather to pray as our work day begins.

We beg God to send the abortion-minded women to us. We pray for all the clients who will call or walk through our doors. We ask that, in a special way, each client would see Jesus through us. The quality and dedication of the women and men who staff the center is awesome and humbling.

Sis, you know I have counseled before, but this is the first time I have worked with women in crisis pregnancies. Often, as I enter a room with a client and make small talk to get the conversation started, I am reminded of what is really taking place at the moment.

In the natural, physical realm, a very frightened, vulnerable young woman is hoping against hope that the

pregnancy test will be negative. She fears her whole life
will be turned upside down. Her past actions race before
her as she confronts the possibility of an unplanned pregnancy. Being pregnant is not just a fearful thought—in a
few short minutes, it could be a reality. The tension in
the air is certainly real!

Yet there is also another reality—a hidden, spiritual
one. As I sit down, I take a deep breath, whispering,
"Jesus, it's you and me."

Often I remember that the angels and saints of heaven
fill that room as a cheering section. Hebrews 12:1, "We
are surrounded by so great a cloud of witnesses," (RSV)
flashes through my mind.

Who knows what's been going on behind the scenes in
this young woman's life? Perhaps her friends and family
have been praying for her to move closer toward accept-
ing the Father's unconditional love. Perhaps she's been
running from God and spiritual things. Today, she has
found her way into a Christian, pro-life pregnancy center
for more than a pregnancy test. What a miracle!

Those of us in Christian centers know what a privilege
it is to watch God's working in so many who are lost. The
Lord gives us a chance to be used as vessels of his love
during their moment of crisis.

Sis, the above background is to set the stage for
the personal experience that opened my eyes to the spiritual realities of helping the women who walk into our
centers.

Two or three times, while counseling an abortion-
minded young woman, I've had an unusual picture
imprinted on my mind. It happened again today, even
though I'm sitting listening and talking to this woman,
it's as if I can "see" the tiny baby inside her!

The baby is facing me with a smile on its face, waving
its arms as if cheering me on. This little one is saying to
me, "Keep talking to Mom, don't give up, keep loving
her. She's so scared—keep loving her so I'll have a chance
to live!"

In reflecting on this, I find myself saying, "Why should I be surprised?" That little child inside does have a spirit and must sense that the pregnancy center is a place where the love of Jesus prevails. The child already knows the mother's anxious and fearful state. But when Mom walks into a Christian setting, the presence of Jesus is tangible. The little one inside now has hope and something to cheer about! Hallelujah!

This mental picture has given me great courage to continue working in the marketplace where women are hurting and babies' lives are being threatened.

Scripture tells us, "Encourage one another daily, as long as it is called Today" (Heb. 3:13). Sis, thanks for your constant encouragement. Pray for us in our ministry.

And thanks for listening.

2

Mom's Solution

Dear Sis,

It's letter-writing time again. Last month I was excited and encouraged about crisis pregnancy center work. The awareness of that unborn baby in the womb who cheers me on to love his or her mother during her time of crisis still overwhelms me.

But today is a different story. To be honest, this work is hard, and at times very frustrating. One type of phone call at the pregnancy center can really do me in. When I hear a voice saying, "My fifteen-year-old daughter is pregnant and I want to have it taken care of," everything in me screams, "No, No, No!"

Yet I try to contain myself, to use my phone counseling skills and continue.

"Your fifteen-year-old daughter is pregnant and you want to have it taken care of?" Often, the mother's response is, "Yes, she's too young to have a baby. I want to make an appointment for an abortion!"

This kind of call is the hardest one for me to deal with emotionally. I do my best to try to get mother and daughter into the pregnancy center to talk. Often you can almost picture the older woman sitting there with the phone book, making a list of places to call for the best "arrangements." Most of them don't come for appointments and you rarely get a chance to know what had happened in those families.

Sis, I see many pregnant young women in crisis. They are panic-stricken, confused, and swayed by the influential people and circumstances surrounding them. My heart goes out to that young woman who feels forced into an abortion. With God's help, we do all we can to love, educate, and enable her to choose life for herself and her baby.

The mother who decides the fate of her daughter (young mama) and her baby is a different dilemma. Young mama may never know there are pregnancy centers to offer alternatives to "mom's solution." Mom makes all the arrangements, including whether dad or granddad is told.

After the phone call, my angry self wants to lash out at mom and say, "Mom, you should know better; mom, you're killing your own grandchild and signing over your daughter to problems that never end; mom, when you help your daughter kill her child, what does that say about your caring for her?"

And the list of condemning phrases goes on.

But then the little voice of the Holy Spirit tugs at my heart to whisper, "You're forgetting—I love that mom. I shed my blood and died for mom, young mama, and that baby in the womb—just as I died for you."

My anger melts into a plea for God's mercy: "Lord Jesus Christ, Son of the living God, have mercy on me, a sinner. Lord, you died for me while I was doing my own thing. Father, please forgive them; they don't know what they're doing. Forgive them as you've forgiven me."

Lord, now I understand. You had that mother call so I could intercede for both of them. O Lord, have mercy. Remove the fear and panic that drives and blinds. Lord, I could be that mother feeling forced to decide that the only solution is abortion. I, too, am capable of that violence. Lord, except for your grace, that could easily be me.

O Lord, I need your mercy, your grace, your love. This mother, daughter, and baby—the whole family—needs you desperately. Lord, forgive my sins; forgive the sins of this family; forgive the sins of the medical profession, the church, the media, the government, the community—the whole world.

Lord, without you we are hopelessly lost. Teach me to intercede for the whole human family of God. Lord, you told us, "If my people who are called by my name humble themselves, and pray and seek my face, and turn from their wicked ways, then I will hear from heaven, and will forgive their sin and heal their land" (2 Chron. 7:14 RSV).

Lord, thank you for this woman's call.

And Sis, thanks for listening.

3

Prayer

Dear Sis,

I told you before what a gift it is to work with praying people. I first learned to pray when I was young, but I still feel like such an infant when it comes to prayer. I guess I am a slow learner—but God still keeps trying to teach me.

Several months after I started here, a very unusual incident took place. When I arrived at the center that morning I saw a couple talking in the hallway. Two volunteers were inside and opening up for business. We sat down in the counseling room to pray, when someone walked in. The receptionist went out to be of assistance. It was the couple I had seen in the hallway. They were looking for the women's clinic that performed abortions. (About a year before, the abortion clinic moved from upstairs to another location.) The receptionist tried offering all of our services, but the couple "had an appointment," so they left.

The receptionist came in and sat down, and we tried again to pray. I couldn't concentrate, so I jumped up and said, "Maybe they're hanging around the hall. I'll be right back, pray for me." I looked out in the parking lot and down the hallway. Then they appeared from the other side of the elevators. They came back to look at the listing of offices in the building. I could see the old, yellow-pages ad in their hands.

I started a conversation with them, and they again mentioned the clinic they were looking for. I asked if we could help—did they need a pregnancy test?

"No."

I added, "It sounds like you're headed for an abortion."

"Yes, we have an appointment for one this morning," she replied.

I asked them, "Do you know what kind of abortion you're having for how pregnant you are?"

At that the young woman, who hadn't yet looked me in the eyes, stared at me and said, "Yes, I'm a nurse and he's a doctor; we know what we're doing. Joe, let's get out of here."

They left. He escorted her to the car. I watched him use the pay phone outside to call for directions to the clinic.

Stunned, angry, and upset, I walked back into the pregnancy center. My volunteers had heard the interchange. The receptionist tried to console me with "You really tried." The counselor verbalized her feelings of helplessness: "We know they are headed over there for an abortion right now. A baby is going to die, and we know the aftermath for them, yet here we sit."

I turned to the counselor and said, "Joyce, are you ready to go?"

"Go where?"

"Go over to the clinic. I can't sit here and do nothing," I exclaimed.

"What are we going to do?" Joyce asked.

"I don't know, but we have to do something!"

We quickly picked up a few pamphlets and educational supplies and drove to the clinic. Our plan was to look for them first in the parking lot; maybe we could start a conversation with them before they entered the clinic.

Sure enough, as we drove past the clinic, the couple sat talking in their car. We parked between them and the

clinic, waiting for them to emerge, and we started praying silently. After about a minute of praying in the spirit,
I said out loud, "In the name of Jesus, I take authority
over you, Satan, and over all your attempts to destroy
that mother and child!"

No sooner had I finished those words when their car
started up and they pulled out of the parking lot!

In our car—silence! We just sat there in awe of what
had just happened; we couldn't believe it! But then I felt
the Lord whisper, "Why should you be surprised?"

I hit the steering wheel and blurted, "Joyce, all we did
was pray; we didn't even have to get out of the car. That
baby, mom, and dad have another chance."

I don't know if she ever had the abortion. I probably
won't know till I get to heaven. But from that day on I've
asked the Lord with more intensity, "Teach me to pray. I
don't want to do this in my own strength. I want to do it
your way!"

Isaiah 64:4 says, "[God] works for those who wait for
him" (RSV). I know my tendency to run ahead of the Lord
and get too busy. I plan this and that and say, "Lord, bless
it!" Then I wonder why it doesn't bear fruit.

For years I've heard that old line, "Heaven helps those
who help themselves." I recently read a better one: "God
helps not those who help themselves, but he is the cham-
pion of those who *cannot* help themselves and of those
who are wise enough not to try."

I can't stop abortion. I can't minister to pregnant
women in crisis or to families caught in the wake of
abortion trauma. I'm not the savior of this sinful, broken
world.

But Sis, I've given my heart to Jesus and said, "Use me,
live your life through me, and let's do the work the Father
assigned for us. Teach me how to pray, how to wait on
you, how to listen until you give marching orders to do
this or that. Teach me to be obedient to your call on
my life and not to worry about what others are or are
not doing."

I recently heard the minister of a church that was deeply in debt say, "We've knocked on many doors that haven't opened. But as we waited on God; he opened doors that no one could close."

Lord, teach me to lean on you as I learn. Obedience, discipline, intercession, spiritual warfare are tough subjects, but I have the Master Teacher inside. Together he and I are a majority!

P.S. Sis, I just heard some great news:

1. Thirty-one churches have joined the twenty-four-hour prayer watch at the Supreme Court, praying for the abortion law to be changed. And they're aiming to set up watches in each state.

2. Some Christians in Arizona walked around two abortion clinics praying quietly like the Israelites as they marched around Jericho's walls. In two weeks each clinic closed.

See Sis, prayer does work! Hallelujah!

4

Married Couples

Dear Sis,

Sis, pregnancy is a strange phenomenon. Can you imagine the following scenario? A missed period, possibly morning sickness, weight gain—little indicators that something different is going on in the body. A urine test, blood test, pelvic examination, and a stranger confirms the diagnosis: "You are pregnant."

"I'm what?"

"You are pregnant, you're going to have a baby."

"I don't *feel* a baby inside of me—maybe you've made a mistake."

Dr. Smith: "Jenny, let's start from the beginning. You're a woman and you've been having menstrual periods for seven years. Physically you are able to bear children. You had intercourse with your husband. One of his up to five hundred million sperm penetrated one of your eggs. That event began a new life.

"Now you are eight weeks past that point. During these past weeks your body has prepared a soft bed in the uterus for optimum growth. Your body has begun to adapt to feeding and protecting another person living inside. Your blood volume has increased, your heart rate is up, your blood pressure has changed, and your kidneys are working more efficiently to carry off the baby's waste products as well as yours. Changes have occurred in every organ system in your body. So far you haven't experienced much in the way of morning sickness or appetite changes, but your chart indicates you have gained three pounds since your last visit. These are examples of how your body has automatically responded to the presence of that preborn child."

Jenny: "It's so hard to believe, but I guess it's true. What's happening to the baby? How big is it? What's it look like?"

Dr. Smith: "The baby inside is one-and-a-third inches long from head to buttocks. He or she has arms, legs, fingers, toes, mouth, nose, ears, and a functioning brain. Technically, the name changes to 'fetus' at eight weeks. The first real bone cells replace cartilage. The little one inside begins to kick his or her feet and move around this week. All body systems are present, and the face and form are definitely human. Everything is now present that will be present in this little one on his or her birth day. The baby weighs less than an ounce and looks like this picture. See the spinal cord, facial features, arms and legs, and internal organs?

You will feel movement in several weeks. You'll notice a twinge—like an arm or leg moving, or maybe a flip-flop as the baby does a somersault in the amniotic sac. Right now you have the signs of missed periods and weight gain. The blood test showed positive for a hormone, HCG; that also points to pregnancy. Also the pelvic examination I just did showed your uterus is soft and large—the size of an eight-week-pregnant uterus."

Jenny: "Doc, can I take some pamphlets and pictures with me? This is a real surprise. I'm still in shock. I want to show my husband."

So Jenny goes home and begins to ponder what she has just learned. "I'm pregnant. I'm gonna have a baby. I wonder if it's a boy or a girl. Will it look like Dave or me? I hope Dave's as excited. . . . We'll have to make plans."

As Dave comes home, Jenny has prepared a special dinner—candlelight—the works! She even sets an extra place. As Dave notices the third place setting he inquires, "Are we having company?" "Yes, we have a guest; he or she will be arriving in about seven months!"

"He or she—arriving in seven months—Jen are you pregnant?"

"Yes, we're gonna have a baby!"

Dave pushes himself from the table and stands to announce, "We're *not* gonna have a baby! I told you I didn't want to have kids so soon. Maybe in a couple of years, but not now. You'll have to have an abortion."

Sis, Jenny comes to us in a whirlwind—pregnant, bewildered, devastated, Dave's word ringing in her ears: *abortion!*

As Jenny recounts her story, my heart goes out to her. She's so hurt and needy. Her whole world has been turned upside-down. Crisis pregnancies happen for married people, too.

Sis, Jenny's story is fiction. But it's similar to a number of stories of married women coming through the pregnancy center. Or sometimes it's the woman who is bent on abortion and the husband, who loves kids, is never told of the pregnancy until after the abortion.

I guess that, being single, I tend to put married couples on a pedestal. I think of mom and dad struggling to provide for us when we were little. They always got so excited about little babies; I can't imagine dad's not wanting another child. I remember his comment, "God only gave us four." Each of us knew we were special.

Both married and single people can have crisis pregnancies. Lord, I pray for each client who calls or enters our doors. May they come to know you whom their hearts seek. May they hunger to know your personal plan for their lives.

Sis, thanks for listening.

5

Laughter

Dear Sis,

I know you worry about me at times—you think I take life too seriously. And it's true that working in the midst of life and death can be overwhelming. In fact, just recently a volunteer (herself excitedly pregnant) walked in, plopped herself in a chair, and burst into tears. "Another client who wants to abort—I can't take this talk of death," she sobbed. I listened and realized once again how depressing this job can become for caring hearts.

Once this volunteer talked and cried, of course, she felt much better, able once again to face the tasks before her. A smile returned to her face—and smiles are so important to balance the heaviness of work like ours.

But today I want to talk about more than smiles. I want to tell you about laughter—those unsought times when peals of delight break forth as gifts from heaven.

Aspects of this work remind me of the wild and crazy things I witnessed as a Physician's Assistant in an emergency room. Sometimes laughter is the only way to break the tension. And besides, dealing with very personal matters such as bodily functions just seems to bring out the funny side of human nature. In our center, talking with people about their sexual habits and dealing with urine specimens can be unforgettable—and hilarious—experiences.

Last January, for instance, at the appreciation luncheon for our volunteers, we had skits for entertainment. And by far the most knee-slapping, rib-holding act was the "Parade of Specimens." Behind the counter stood a "receptionist" receiving "clients" and taking their specimens for the free pregnancy test.

Client #1 arrived with a quart Mason jar full of urine and the statement, "I hope this is enough!" (Only a few drops of urine are needed!)

Client #2 approached the counter with a returnable Pepsi™ bottle. The receptionist looked hard at the narrow neck and wondered, "How did she get the urine in there? Will she ask for the bottle back?"

Client #3 snuck up to the counter, sheepishly looked around, and then produced a large McDonald's™ french fry container with a little jar inside. She added, "I didn't want people to suspect anything." (As each client arrived, the uncontrollable laughter from the staff held up the performance.)

Client #4 walked to the counter with a large pickle jar and announced, "I cleaned the jar, but I'm not sure if I got out the smell." (We've never seen a pickle jar of urine that didn't smell like pickles. Sometimes the contents even *look* like pickle juice!)

Client #5 slowly appeared holding at arm's length a leaking paper bag, which she gently placed on the counter. Her explanation: "I guess the paper cup inside has a leak."

Howls of laughter, loud cackles, and tears of joy told us how good it is to look at the funny side.

Of course, we can't laugh out loud when clients come in nervous and afraid and act out one of the above five scenarios. (They really happen!) Instead, the specimens are placed solemnly on the lab counter, and we begin the test. If another volunteer enters and sees the cause for laughter, a "knowing glance and a smile" are exchanged until the crisis situation is passed. Then the laughter breaks out later, in the privacy of the conference room.

Another source of chuckles is new volunteers who are learning and trying hard to do things well. A volunteer—we'll call her Mary—was doing her first solo interview of a client. She had started the pregnancy test and picked up her clipboard to fill out the Client Information Sheet. The top of the form contains the standard questions: name, address, phone number, date, occupation, marital status, age, race, religion, and "How did you hear about us?"

Mary, trying to hide her nervousness, asked the question, "race?" The client waited until Mary looked up before saying, "I think I'm black." Both grinned, then laughed hysterically. Mary and the gang at work that day will never forget "I think I'm black."

I believe that God likes to bless us with little gems along the way like laughter—and hugs! The volunteers like to tease me about drafting others to help with little projects at the center. They also like to see if I'll forget to give them a hug when they arrive. The *Hug Therapy* book and poster (Kathleen Keating, Minneapolis: Comp Care Publications, 1983) are reminders that Jesus has given us another way to reach out to each other. I've yet to see someone turn down a little hug. Sis, I am grateful for the hugs and kisses you've given me over the years! I send you a special hug today!

Sometimes the fellowship and the laughter go together. Recently two of our board members went to an AAI Conference. (AAI is Alternatives to Abortion International—the network of emergency pregnancy services.) Though both of them had worked at the center for a while, they had never had a chance to really get to know one another.

The first night at the conference, they decided to go to bed early. But once the lights were out, the conversation—and the laughter—started. Each one topped the other with stories of funny things that had happened to them and their families. Soon their giggles were uncontrollable; they thought that someone would surely complain about the noise. Finally, two hours later, they went to sleep, with sides and cheeks sore from nonstop riotous howling.

These two women in their forties and fifties returned from three days of working and playing together like little kids coming home from their first overnight. Both were well aware that the seriousness of the conference and the continuous burden of heavy issues had been offset by the comic relief of that night and the joy of getting to know each other. And they will never forget that trip.

Sis, the last experience I want to share is one that happens every day, when we pray together as a staff. We have many different styles of prayer and singing. But often there is a pregnant pause, a holy silence, and a smile will come across my face—sometimes other faces, too. It's as if we sense that God is smiling at us. The same Jesus who rose from the dead, laughing at the victory over his enemy, Satan, now rejoices over us. Our God rejoices over us with singing. The prophet Zephaniah described this same delight of the Lord:

> The Lord your God is with you,
>   he is mighty to save.
> He will take great delight in you,
>   he will quiet you with his love,
>   he will rejoice over you with singing.
>   Zeph. 3:17

What a humbling honor to sense the presence of our Lord and King laughing, delighting in us.

Yeah, Sis, the work is serious, even morbid at times. But, oh the joy! Praise God for his gift of laughter.

Thanks for listening.

6

Discouragement

Dear Sis,

Today I am struck with a problem that surfaces regularly in this work. John Powell says it well: "I think that, if I were the devil, I would dangle two temptations in the pro-life line of vision. The first temptation would be discouragement. I would remind pro-life people that they are a small minority, a lonely voice crying in the wilderness. The second temptation I would propose to the beautiful pro-life persons would be overresponsibility." Today, I need to talk about discouragement, someday I will mention overresponsibility (*To Rescue the Future*, Dave Andrusko, ed. [Toronto: Life Cycle Books], pp. 285–86).

Sis, dealing with discouragement is a real issue for volunteers with big hearts. The women and men who arrive at the door of the pregnancy centers hear an inner call to get involved. Being verbally opposed to abortion, staying home and saying, "Ain't it awful," is no longer an option. Their convictions about the incredible worth of the preborn child in the womb and the plight of the fearful pregnant woman mobilizes their energies to action. The majority of the volunteers have great gifts of mercy and compassion. They have tender hearts for the

34

wounded, the suffering, and the oppressed. Often they
weep with those who weep and are ready to lend a hand, a
tissue, a hug, or whatever seems to help.

A young woman walks in looking for a free pregnancy
test and maybe a kind face. As she is made comfortable
and her history taken, her fear and tension are dimin-
ished. Often a real connection develops between the volunteer and the client. She knows she's being listened to
and loved just as she is.

So when that same young woman gets up and states,
"Thanks for everything, but I'm still going to have
an abortion next week," it's so, so hard for the volunteer
who cares. After investing a lot of energy in listening, caring, educating, and consoling a stranger—now a
friend—in distress, it's devastating to hear those words.
Racing thoughts prevail: "What happened?" "What did I
do wrong?" "Oh, she will suffer so much if she goes
through with that abortion she really doesn't want!" For
the volunteer who has tried the very best and now feels
failure, who knows the horror of the abortion experience
for the baby and the long-term suffering for the mother,
the experience can be crushing.

"One point six million abortions per year in this country—what can I do? I thought I could help make a difference, but I can't even be successful one-on-one with a
woman headed for an abortion." Discouragement, hope-
lessness, and despair can descend like crashing waves on
the shore.

Sis, I remember the day a middle-aged volunteer,
Jackie, was going through the current client file and saw
the name of a teenager in her neighborhood. This girl had
played with Jackie's own kids all their lives. The girl's
parents were good friends and neighbors and active
church participants; in fact, they had even done some
volunteer work for our pregnancy center. And yet the file
showed that the girl was abortion-minded.

Jackie wept for the girl and her family. And she wept
for her own kids, wondering whether they might be

headed for abortions while their mom is doing pro-life work in the community. Jackie battled great feelings of discouragement because of that experience.

I also remember the day Sally mentioned a client, Ruth, with whom she had talked several times. After their talks, Ruth had decided to carry her baby to term. "But then," Sally told me, "I called Ruth just to say hi. And Ruth cussed me out, said she was headed for an abortion, and hung up." Later that day, Sally's husband found her on her bed crying. When he asked what was wrong, all she could say at the time was, "It hurts so much to care for that mom and her baby." Sally knew that afternoon that Jesus was weeping with her. That sense of powerlessness to do more, say more, or pray more can be so discouraging at times.

Jesus had a similar experience with the rich young man mentioned in the Gospels. The two had a wonderful conversation, and Jesus really loved him. But that rich young man couldn't bring himself to give away his wealth and follow Jesus; the Scriptures say that his face fell and he went away sad. And Jesus had to allow the man to choose freely to follow him or not. Jesus didn't run after the man and offer to change the demands to make it easier. Instead, Jesus painfully let the rich young man choose (see Mark 10:17–22).

What a lesson for us in our work! God allows people to choose death for our babies and great suffering for themselves and others. No matter what our sin—God permits us to separate ourselves from him. If he didn't, our choosing him wouldn't really mean anything.

So, Sis, how do we deal with this great temptation to discouragement? By remembering that "love never fails," and that God doesn't command us to be successful with everyone we meet. Yet he does expect us to be faithful in loving each one as he has so lavishly loved us—unconditionally. The only way I can attempt to do this is to keep my eyes on Jesus and his faithfulness and not on the circumstances that sway me to think God has checked out. Jesus never fails, his love in us never fails. Someday we will see the fruits of our labor. But meanwhile we need to cling to the God of all comfort and encouragement.

Dear Father, you know the feelings, the struggles, and the hearts of all volunteers in pro-life work. Help us to surrender our need for success to you, to allow you to live and love through us. May the disappointments and heartaches drive us to you. Enable us to receive your courage and strength to care for others as you have gently and tenderly cared for us.

Thanks, Lord, for hearing the cry of our hearts.

Sis, thanks again for being there.

7

Adoption

Dear Sis,

One client I'm working with now is really in a pickle. Her six-week-old baby is in foster care, ready to be adopted. The father of the baby, who disappeared for most of the pregnancy, has just called to say, "I'm not releasing for adoption." Time will tell what happens. We're doing lots of praying for God's best for all concerned.

Sis, I have such mixed feelings about adoption. To be honest, I doubt I could ever release a child of mine for adoption. And yet:

My first cousin is adopted;

Several good friends have released for adoption;

A couple of friends are adopted;

Several friends of mine have adopted children and are encouraging me to adopt as a single woman;

I've run groups for adoptive parents;

I've prayed with adopted children;

Promoting the option of adoption to volunteers, clients, and the community is an everyday experience for me;

We are each adopted children of our heavenly Father.

Sis, life isn't simple. Two million couples in this country are eagerly waiting to adopt a child. One point six million babies are aborted each year. Common sense says, "Why not take the would-be-aborted babies and give them to the couples waiting for kids?" How we wish it were that simple!

Couples who want to adopt go to incredible lengths to have a child. Often they have:

tried unsuccessfully for years to have their own children,

investigated different types of adoption,

invested great time, money, and emotional energy into preparing for adoption.

Their joy and gratitude at receiving this long-awaited boy or girl is unparalleled. They have a special sense that this one child has been hand-picked by God and entrusted into their care for a time—a treasure to handle with tender loving care.

We have couples writing and calling, hoping in vain that we handle private adoptions. Ads in the newspapers and magazines appear regularly from parents desperate to adopt.

Sis, you probably already know that side of the story. But I need to talk about a couple of the other sides, too.

Soon after I started in this work, I met with a young woman, a college student who had been on her way up the steps to the abortion clinic when her sister had intercepted her. Two days later, she had made another appointment for an abortion which was never kept. A few days later another sister brought her into our center. Connie was tough, scared, trying to hold it all together. She said, "Tell me about abortion." I put on my clinical physician's assistant manner and described a suction abortion procedure to her simply and straightforwardly.

I could see that, behind her tough shell, Connie was nauseated by the details I described. When I finished, she said, "Tell me about adoption." I proceeded, gently, asking her questions about her situation. Soon I heard her say, "I couldn't live with myself knowing I killed my baby. Adoption is something I can live with, I think."

In that grace-filled hour, I watched God change Connie's heart. That encounter was the beginning of a special friendship between Connie and me. She moved out of town to live with one of her sisters for most of the pregnancy, but we kept in touch somewhat through letters and phone calls. She landed in a Bible study with other women in crisis pregnancies. And little by little she started letting God into her life. I saw her once toward the end of the pregnancy, and she was truly one of those radiant pregnant women. And her spiritual growth was obvious; that hard shell had completely disappeared. Her self-esteem was increasing daily. Her attitude toward the father of the baby, her parents, and others was greatly changed. Resentment and unforgiveness were evaporating.

I surprised Connie and the family by arriving at the hospital just after little John was born. What a celebration at his entry into this world! The next day, Connie and I shared and cried, prayed and hugged as we took turns holding John. Holding that perfect little guy stirred up all kinds of thoughts and feelings:

You're beautiful, and you look so much like your father.

You came so close to being aborted.

What a plan God must have for your life!

Your adoptive parents will be so excited.

Your mommy has grown so much because of you.

How your mommy loves you!

Connie is the first to admit what carrying and delivering John did for her in taking responsibility for her actions for the first time. Connie feels sure that, had she aborted, her lifestyle would have stayed on the same self-destructive course.

But, Sis, Connie also talks about how real the grieving was after she came home from the hospital. She was surprised and confused at the pain. She worked through the sadness and empty arms, but she admits to thoughts that reoccur:

What is John doing now?

What does he look like?

What would my life have been like if I kept him?

Will John and I ever meet?

I hope he has special birthdays.

Will he understand and love me?

I bet his adoptive parents are so happy.

Connie believes that God has healed a lot of her hurts already—and the healing will continue. She sees the pain of her postadoption grieving as a positive experience. The devastation of postabortion trauma had she decided otherwise is beyond her comprehension. She's worked hard and saved money to return to college in a couple of months. She also has helped us at the pregnancy center. When I see what God has done in Connie's life in two years through a crisis pregnancy and adoption, I stand speechless.

Sis, Connie and I prayed for John not to experience the identity problems and wounded spirit that sometimes plague an adopted child. Paula Sandford's booklet, "New Life for your Adopted Child," (Coeur d'Alene, ID: Elijah House, Inc., 1982) helped me to see how to pray for God's healing for those coming through crisis pregnancies.

Little Johnny has every chance to grow whole and healthy. I like what Anne Kiemel Anderson writes in *And with the Gift Came Laughter* (Wheaton, IL: Tyndale, 1978, p. 61). "People need to know . . . adopted children need to be taught . . . that for most birth mothers, giving up a baby is not an act of rejection, it is the most selfless, courageous, brave deed they can do. It is laying aside their own desires and longings, to bestow on that baby something greater and better than they can provide. . . . Never yet have I met a birth mother who thoughtlessly gave her baby away."

Sis, thanks for listening.

8

Almost Aborted

Dear Sis,

I wonder how many people walking around were almost aborted during their nine-month journey in their mother's womb.

I am stunned by the clinical experience of a psychiatrist, Dr. Andrew Feldmar, who was cited in *Healing the Greatest Hurt* (Matthew and Dennis Linn and Sheila Fabricant [NY: Paulist Press, 1985], p. 113). Dr. Feldmar had three patients who tried to kill themselves at the same time each year. The dates seemed meaningless until Dr. Feldmar realized that each of these patients was attempting suicide at a time which would be the anniversary of their second or third month in the womb. When he investigated their histories, he discovered that the dates of the suicide attempts were the dates when each one's mother had attempted an abortion. Not only was the timing of each patient's suicide attempt reminiscent of an abortion attempt, but even the method was similar. One patient whose mother had tried to abort him with a darning needle tried suicide with a razor blade. Another, whose mother had used chemicals, tried suicide with a drug overdose. When Dr. Feldmar's patients realized that their suicidal ideas were really memories of their mothers' attempts to kill them, they were freed from the compulsion to commit suicide.

Dr. Feldmar's conclusion was that those preborn children at less than three months in the womb received the message, "You're not wanted; you deserve to die." Though they were never actually told this once they had been born, the message kept repeating itself: "You're not wanted; you deserve to die." Sis, what a powerful eye-opener this is for me.

There is much we don't know about experiences in the womb affecting later life. Understanding how impressions are received and stored prenatally keeps researchers very busy. But evidence is mounting that prebirth experiences *do* affect us in later life.

Recently I counseled and prayed with a woman, Betsy, who knew that her mother had tried to abort her more than once. She escaped two abortion attempts and a near fatal accident and arrived in this world at three pounds. Betsy's mom had never tried to hide the fact that Betsy was an unwelcomed war baby with an unknown father. The oldest of six children, Betsy felt she always had to work at being accepted. Seeking approval from others became a way of life for her.

At age twenty-two, Betsy had her own crisis pregnancy, which resulted in a baby girl she released for adoption. She later married, had a son, and started taking in foster children. Eventually she committed her life to Jesus and grew strong spiritually, but one area remained out of control: a sharp, hurtful tongue. Somewhere in Betsy was a boiling pot of angry emotions that couldn't be controlled with prayer, Bible study or willpower. Her guilt over verbally lashing out at those she loved—especially at her foster kids, who had been abused enough already—surfaced again and again, but she couldn't seem to stop herself.

Betsy and I agreed to pray and ask God to show her the source of the problem. And surely and gently, God

brought to the surface the angry little Betsy within—
the inner child who didn't understand why she wasn't
wanted, loved, or appreciated; why she had to perform for
approval; why she was rejecting the foster kids around
her, who also were unwanted.

Our time together was a holy time of God's presence
and the illumination of his Holy Spirit on a soul ready to
come out of the darkness into the light of Christ's healing
love. I sensed that God was pouring a healing balm over
Betsy's entire being. She later allowed Jesus to love away
the seething anger.

Isn't it great that our God is not limited by time and
space? He can heal the deepest wounds. He longs to make
us whole and holy in his sight. It was a sacred time of
watching the Holy Spirit do spiritual surgery on Betsy
that day. Forty-plus years of anger are being replaced day
by day by his unconditional love for her.

Sis, I want to end with one more story—this one told to
me by George, an evening volunteer counselor. One night
when George was working, a young lady, Brenda, arrived
for counseling. She had already had a pregnancy test
somewhere; she knew she was pregnant. George asked
her how she had found out about us, and she answered,
"Planned Parenthood"! (Sis, we don't usually get referrals
from Planned Parenthood.)

George asked, "Would you tell me about it?" And
Brenda told this story:

"I am pregnant, my husband has left me, and I thought
I had to abort. I made the appointment with Planned
Parenthood and arrived at the clinic. They gave me some
pamphlets to read and showed me into the examining
room. I was undressed and up on the table, waiting for the
doctor to come in and start the abortion. I put the pamphlets on the floor next to the table I was lying on. I
waited and waited. Then I reached for the literature on
the floor, and behind those pamphlets was a crumpled-up
brochure from this crisis pregnancy center. I opened the

brochure, read it, and decided, I'm leaving this place! I got dressed and left the clinic without talking to anyone. Then I came here. Will you help me like this brochure says?"

Sis, can you believe it? Brenda came so close to aborting—so very close.

I wonder what angel or previous client left that brochure of ours on the floor of the abortion chamber. I wish I knew who else in addition to our people have been praying for Brenda and that baby. Brenda is carrying her baby now. She needs lots of help and support. She's so grateful for that crumpled-up brochure and the grace of God. She keeps talking about what a special child this must be. . . .

And someday we'll talk about praying for healing of that little one's almost abortion.

Sis, miracles do happen!!

PART **Two**

The Pro-Life/
Abortion Arena

9

Sick

Dear Sis,

I'm sick! I feel so bad inside I don't know what to do.

I can hear you saying, "What's wrong? Do you still have the flu?"

No, Sis, I'm over the flu I had a couple weeks ago, but I'm weak and taking some time off to get back on my feet.

I'm out of town for a few days to get well and trying not to think about the mounting work load at the pregnancy center. Working full time in this abortion/pro-life arena is hard for me to turn off when I leave the office. I know I need to rest, yet I also know that more than four thousand babies will die today—one every twenty seconds. The magnitude of those numbers overwhelms me—it's almost beyond my ability to comprehend. I need to be careful I don't fall victim to John Powell's second temptation of "overresponsibility" that I mentioned in an earlier letter. Jesus is still on the throne as King and Lord of all. Ellen doesn't need to play rescuer by taking on all the problems of the world.

But today I'm stunned, angry, and sick over what just happened. I have to get this off my chest.

Being director of a crisis pregnancy center, I've picked up some strange habits. For instance, when I go to new cities, I like to look in the yellow pages under "clinics" and see if I can tell the pro-life centers from the abortion clinics by the way they advertise. I did that today. There was one ad that caught my eye because I wasn't sure whether they were pro-life or pro-abortion. I phoned to see how they would answer typical questions. A middle-aged woman answered the phone, and this is what happened.

Clinic: "Hello, Women's Health Center. Can I help you?"

Ellen: "Um, hi! I'm calling for a friend about your abortions advertised in the yellow pages. . . ."

Clinic: "Has your friend had a pregnancy test yet?"

Ellen: "Yes, it's positive. How much are your abortions?"

Clinic: "Well, it depends. How late is she on her period?"

Ellen: "Oh, I'm not sure. I think she's two to three weeks late."

Clinic: "The fee is one hundred eighty-five dollars if she's a couple of weeks late. We take cash, check, or credit card. We could schedule her for next Tuesday. If she came on her lunch hour, she could probably get back to work in the afternoon. Would you like me to schedule an appointment?"

Ellen: "Um, no. I need some more information first. What about the risks?"

Clinic: "Risks? There are no risks. It's no big deal. It's less risky than going to the dentist. In fact, some people come in for three or four abortions a year. It's just an expensive means of birth control."

Ellen: "What's the procedure? What happens?"

Clinic: "It's just a menstrual extraction of two periods—a little cramping, and she can go to work afterward."

F11-

my Limits
fetal Dev sheet

de. Tissue
h week. It's
ortion just
ey, it's been
a baby inside

really believes
ally hearing this.
with the truth? Do I
I could decide, the

..., I have another call. Can I make
that appointment for your friend?"

Ellen: "No, I'll call you back. . . ."

Sis, I'm still in shock. This conversation really happened! I was dumbfounded as I got off the phone. I jotted down her statements so I wouldn't forget.

This receptionist honestly believes that "no tissue starts forming till twelve weeks." I'm holding in my hand "Precious Preborn," a model of a ten-to-twelve-week-old preborn child. I can see all the fingers and toes, eyes and ears. All the body systems are present, heart waves (EKG) and brain waves (EEG) have been detectable for weeks. Yet I heard this clinic receptionist confidently state, "It's just liquid."

Sis, I know better, but many frightened young women who haven't been exposed to fetal development would believe this receptionist, who sounds so convincing. How many women have been told these lies?

No wonder the horror on women's faces when they see pictures of the preborn child for the first time and blurt out, "I killed my baby! They told me it was a clump of cells, not a fully formed little child!"

How is this ignorance possible in today's educated society? Sis, I'm sick! Here I am trying to recover from a physical illness, and I'm hit smack in the face with the reality of this ugly war. Innocent babies are dying, mothers are being traumatized for life, and the casualties continue to mount.

Lord, if I react this way—how you must grieve over your people! Lord, show me what to do with what I know. How do you want to use me to make a difference? Make my life count!

Thanks for listening.

10

Sharing

Dear Sis,

This work is never dull. Besides the adventures and trials of clients and volunteers in the pregnancy center, part of my job as director involves speaking to groups in the community. Schools, youth groups, parents, professionals, church congregations—each group presents its own set of challenges. Speaking to groups is much different than sharing one-on-one in a counseling room. I always pray for a special touch from God for me and for the group involved. God's anointing for the event makes an incredible difference in lives being changed.

Not long ago, a request arrived from a volunteer to speak at her church youth group. The evening would consist of a Protestant woman pastor speaking in favor of legalized abortion, followed by me presenting the pro-life arguments and explaining what happens at the crisis pregnancy center. Sis, this was a first for me. I had never debated this issue with a member of the clergy!

The night we were to speak, we both sat on the podium as twenty-five young people arrived, with lots of joking and enjoying each other before the evening began. After introductions, the pastor presented first. Her compassion for women caught in crisis was clearly apparent.

Her arguments in favor of legalized abortion were pretty standard, and she presented them very well. As she mentioned the need to abort a mentally or physically handicapped preborn, I felt this sinking feeling in the pit of my stomach; she was arguing effectively for getting rid of God's special kids.

As I began to speak I struggled with a feeling of not being convincing; the pastor's presentation had left its mark. But I went ahead to present the truth about fetal life in the womb, about what happens during an abortion, and about the suffering of some of the women who return for postabortion counseling. I explained details on the services of a pregnancy center and sat down. Quietly I whispered to God: "Help, Lord, make your presence known soon."

Questions and answers followed the break, and at one point the pastor stated again the need to abort genetically deformed kids after an amniocentesis showed problems. A young man in the back raised his hand and said, "We've been studying the Constitution in political science class. It starts, 'We the people are endowed with certain inalienable rights—the right to life, liberty, and the pursuit of happiness.' It doesn't say, 'we the people with all our arms and legs . . .' or 'we the people with an IQ of 120. . .' It says, 'We the people!' How can you decide which people are worthy of living?"

Sis, my eyes filled with tears. That guy had the Constitution and the Declaration of Independence a little mixed up—but what a wonderful thing to say! God showed up that night, and the kids knew the truth when it was spoken. The rest of the discussion was clearly tipped toward the pro-life end of the debate. What an answer to prayer!

Another speaking engagement I will never forget was the January day when I spoke to an all-boy Catholic school. The school officials had asked for a pro-life educational film and speaker to address six hundred predominately black young men, and I had agreed to come. Back at the pregnancy center, everyone was praying for this special opportunity. Introductions to the topic and the film *Assignment Life* covered most of the available hour. During the entire film, you could hear a pin drop in that auditorium. Eyes turned away or mouths dropped in horror on seeing what actually takes place during an abortion. After the film, I had seven minutes to share, and I used the time to focus the issue for my predominantly black audience. (The fact that abortion is a great way to eliminate blacks was news to most of them.) George Grant in *Grand Illusions* (Brentwood, TN.: Wolgemuth and Hyatt Publishers, Inc., 1989) cites a Health and Human Services Administration report that 43 percent of all abortions are performed on blacks and another 10 percent on Hispanics. This, despite the facts that blacks make up only 11 percent of the total U.S. population and Hispanics only about 8 percent. I challenged these young men to stand up for life, to educate themselves and to make a difference in this abortion holocaust.

Sis, I don't even remember much of what I said—I just remember the power—the sense that it was God speaking through me that day. That's all that mattered. This school continues to be a forerunner in educating their students about life and encouraging involvement in their local areas.

Sometimes there are great gifts and wonderful surprises in this high-intensity work. I think you'll remember this story when I refresh your memory. It's one of those stories I need to retell for myself.

One evening I had to return a pro-life film to our local Right-to-Life group. It was a ten to fifteen minute ride up the street, so I asked Jo Anne's kids, Shelly and Jeff, if they wanted to go for a ride to return the film. (They were six and four then.) We piled into the car and chatted on the way. After depositing the film we headed home, and Shelly piped-up, "Let's each sing a song. I'll sing a song,

Jeff will sing a song, and you sing a song." Shelly began with "Old MacDonald." Jeff followed with "B-I-N-G-O." I started, "Jesus, loves Shelly and Jeff, yes He does, yes He does. . ."

Shelly blurted out, "Jesus—he's dead."

"Well, sort of," I replied. "He died, but God raised him up from the dead."

"Where does he live?" Shelly asked.

"He lives in heaven with God and. . ."

". . . My guardian angel?" she added.

"Do you have a guardian angel, Shelly?"

"Yes, his name is Petey."

"What about you, Jeff?"

"Yes, my angel is Jason."

Shelly innocently asked, "What about your guardian angel—what's his name?"

"I don't know, Shelly," I replied.

Assuredly Shelly said, "We'll have to give him a name." She thought and then began, "Petey, Jason, and . . . I know: Sammy. Your guardian angel's name is Sammy."

"Thanks, Shelly; Sammy's a great name. Say, where is your guardian angel, Petey?" I asked.

Shelly quickly responded, "Right here on my lap."

"What about you, Jeff; where's Jason?"

Jeff answered and pointed, "Right there in the back seat."

The conversation ended right there. How I wish I had a tape recording of what had just taken place. Petey, Jason, and Sammy felt as real as we three sitting in the car. Oh, the joy and faith of little children! And such a wonderful treat from heaven to balance the heaviness of the abortion battle.

As always, thanks for listening and being there.

11

Deception

Dear Sis,

Wow! The heat's been turned up in our pro-life/abortion area. Recently articles in the newspapers and a prime-time TV program have again called controversial attention to the pregnancy center. The sensational headline, "Bogus Abortion Clinics," captured the public's attention and turned them toward reading about some pro-life crisis pregnancy centers.

One fact that has emerged through the publicity is that some centers give deceptive answers to the woman who calls looking for an abortion. One approach advocates a "save the baby at any cost" protocol. Counselors are encouraged to lead the caller to believe she can obtain an abortion at the center. This ensures a face-to-face encounter with the young mom.

Every day I see the great temptation of wanting to tell the woman anything just to get her into the center. Each of us thinks, "If she just comes in, I'll have a chance to talk her out of the abortion." Sometimes we forget that only God changes hearts.

Our volunteers are such compassionate, caring people that I often think they would rather die than see that mother and baby undergo an abortion.

Recognizing the temptations and the tender hearts of volunteers, we establish very clear guidelines in training

our phone counselors—and those guidelines include
truthfulness. But more than anything we try to stress
essential listening skills—making sure a warm, friendly,
knowledgeable, and caring voice is reaching through the
phone.

Recently a new volunteer was being quizzed on
"What's the most important thing to remember when
you're answering the phones?" She answered, "That the
caller can hear and feel a smile in your voice and that she
is the most important person in the world right now."
That volunteer-in-training had learned her lesson well.
Still, reaching out in love must be balanced by a recogni-
tion that this caller is entitled to the truth regarding our
services.

Face-to-face counseling with women in crisis also
holds its share of temptations to bend the truth. We guard
against the desire to exaggerate the horrors of abortion by
listing inaccurate facts about the risks and complications
of the medical procedure.

Sis, we both know that abortion is horrible! We don't
even have adequate adjectives to describe abortion and its
ramifications. But as much as we hate abortion, we are
still called by God to be truthful. Our facts and presentation regarding what a woman can expect if she opts for an
abortion must be impeccably honest.

Lying to a woman to persuade her out of an abortion
brings so many problems. You might talk her out of
aborting this particular baby. But how many more lives
might she abort when she realizes she has been manipu-
lated and deceived?

Is a baby's life worth a lie? Does the end justify the
means? The struggle is real. We absolutely hate to see a
woman choose to abort her baby. In our work, the client
who aborts is often interpreted as "I failed." Our hidden
desire as involved volunteers is for success, power, control, and happy endings. We have to be careful not to play
messiah and rescue others with our agendas for them.

It is overwhelming to me that no matter how many bad, rotten, or lethal decisions we make, God never takes away that freedom to choose evil. Knowing he sent his Son Jesus to die for us when we were in the midst of sin and because of sin brings me to my knees.

The woman who has chosen abortion must be loved and cared for with compassion and granted the same dignity that Jesus showed for the greatest of sinners. Sis, at times I sound like a broken record: Except for the grace of God—it could easily be me! Lord, help me to hate the sin, yet love the sinner. Teach me not to judge the hearts of others.

Sis, this is background to share a special blessing with you. About the same time the media items were hotly discussed, our pregnancy center received a great compliment.

A woman in her twenties, a former client, brought in a frightened fourteen-year-old who needed a pregnancy test. The former client had had five abortions and a life of drug abuse. She knows who we are and what we believe about abortions. And yet she was willing to entrust her young teenaged friend to our care—even though she still believes in abortions. Her actions spoke volumes to me about the kind of love she has received from the volunteers in previous visits. Fortunately, the fourteen-year-old was not pregnant, and the former client expressed an interest in postabortion counseling.

My prayer today for the pregnancy center is that each person who enters or calls will be reverenced and valued as a child of the Father. Lord, make us empty vessels through which you can pour your great love and truth to a broken, hurting world. Father, get our eyes off success and onto faithfulness and obedience. We hunger to hear your words: "Well done, good and faithful servant. I've seen how you love one another. Enter into my kingdom."

Sis, thanks for listening.

12

Repentance

Dear Sis,

I have a heavy burden on my heart: *Repentance*—that big word makes most people cringe and feel guilty. I know I need to understand it more from God's point of view.

I recently heard a pastor on the radio talking about abortion. He called attention to the Christians active in the pro-life movement who condemn other Christians and the rest of the country for not stopping the evil of abortion. It's easy for active pro-lifers to condemn not only the doctors who perform abortions, the politicians and judges who rule in favor of abortion, and anyone connected with the industry, but also anyone who doesn't approach the problem exactly like we do. There seems to be this insatiable urge to be on the "right side," to be on the winning team. We want to mock and say, "I'm right and you're wrong," on so many levels of communication.

Sis, remember when I taught high school? I often showed a great little film, "Is It Always Right to Be Right?" It depicted an earth divided on how to be successful; each side insisting they were right, the other side wrong, and the two worlds moved further apart from each other. As the division continued, all color and activity on earth stopped.

Finally, after months of a very bleak, sterile existence, someone on side one sent a message to side two: "I may be wrong!"

Everyone else on side one was shocked at such a thought. "That can't be; we're always right!" Side two laughed hilariously at the message, yet returned a note: "You may be right!" That was the beginning of honest communication, and the two worlds began to work toward a "declaration of interdependence!" They began to live out the slogan, "We don't have it all together—but together we have it all."

My heart aches when I see what's happening among strong pro-life leaders. This one doesn't talk to that one. Don't mention certain names in certain company! Large, powerful groups squabble over such issues as: how to change abortion laws, what stand to take on birth control, and how to reconcile differing religious approaches. In some Christian pro-life circles, evangelicals outlaw Catholics; Catholics are threatened by charismatics. We are killing each other from within!

Sis, Satan's no slouch—his same old "divide and conquer" tactics are working just fine. He wants to keep us focused on other people's faults or weaknesses and thus distract us from the real battle, which is against the spiritual powers that come to steal, kill, and destroy all life.

I read an interesting statement in David Augsburger's book, *Caring Enough to Hear and Be Heard* (Scottsdale, PA.: Herald Press, 1982). He writes, "Although it may seem strange at first hearing, most difficulties arise not from our differences, but from our similarities. Our differences often attract, complete, complement each other; our similarities grate, irritate, and frustrate us. When a fault in you provokes anger in me, then I know that your fault is my fault, too" (pp. 18, 20).

The pastor on the radio made a similar point. He was remarking how Christians who jump on the pro-life bandwagon tend to become incredibly self-righteous: "Well, of course, God is on our side." Sis, I knew he was speaking to me as he shared the story from Joshua 5. Before the taking of Jericho, Joshua approached a stranger who was standing nearby with sword drawn. "Are you for us or for our enemies?" Joshua asked. (I could easily hear "Are you for or against abortion?")

The man with the sword answered, "Neither . . . but as commander of the army of the Lord I have now come. . . . Take off your sandals, for the place where you are standing is holy."

This man of God wasn't for either side, for both sides were wrong—one in principle, the other in attitude. Often we point the finger at other people who we think should be doing more to stop abortion when we are guilty, too. By my silence and inactivity for years, I allowed the evil of abortion to grow. I am the guilty one. I am a voting citizen who elects representatives with my values to office. When did I start being concerned with moral and family issues of politicians? I am responsible for this country's mistakes. I can't blame or criticize anyone else.

Sis, you've heard me say it before: Except for God's grace, I'd still be closing my eyes to the problems rather than becoming part of the solution.

In other words, I need to repent. I need to acknowledge my sin of omission and commission personally. Lord, where have I failed you and your Word? Where have I allowed a prejudice for "my way of doing things" or "my church is the right one" to distract me from your real purposes?

Lord, forgive me. Forgive the United States for our national sins—especially the shedding of innocent blood. Lord, we know that violence begets violence, that only our heartfelt repentance and your forgiveness can free us from the certain disaster we face without you. Lord, forgive us for we know not what we do.

Lord, you've told us, "If my people, who are called by my name, will humble themselves and pray and seek my face and turn from their wicked ways, then I will hear from heaven and forgive their sin and will heal their land" (2 Chron. 7:14).

Lord, we pray for a healthy, balanced awareness of guilt and nonguilt to be able to repent of our sin on every level. Thank you for your endless mercy, Lord.

Well, Sis, I guess I got carried away again.

Thanks for listening, anyway.

13

Birth Control

Dear Sis,

If you want a smooth, easygoing, noncontroversial job, don't work in a pregnancy center. Great emotions are aroused when words like *pregnancy, miscarriage, adoption,* and *abortion* are mentioned. Everyone has his or her own definitions, experiences, and feelings about each of these.

Teen pregnancy, especially, gets people worked up. The media focuses tremendous attention on this issue. Various programs, resolutions, and task forces are discussed at federal, state, and local school levels. And most of the discussion seems to center on solving the teenage pregnancy problem through educating about contraception and making birth-control devices available to teens. You've heard it, "safe-sex."

Sis, the issue of birth control for teenagers causes more fights than abortion. What a mess!

Some pro-abortion advocates are uncomfortable with legalized abortion but see it as a necessary evil. Their view is that "unwanted pregnancies happen, and it's better to abort in a safe, sterile environment than to have illegal back alley abortions. But after that, be sure to get them on birth control so that it doesn't happen again."

64

I heard the same argument from another angle while on vacation this summer. I was taking pictures at a scenic overlook, and a man and his wife offered to take a picture of me and my friend. Afterward, a conversation started among the four of us. When he realized the nature of my work, he expressed strong feelings about the issue. He said, "I'm a Christian, and I'm against abortion, but let's get them on birth control."

Sis, I was grateful he was a Christian and against abortion. But I was saddened by what I see as lack of understanding about birth control, young people, and God's plan for us and our sexuality. This lack of understanding is a common occurrence among most adults in today's society.

In the years that the birth-control pill has been available, in the seventeen years since abortion on demand has been legalized, there has been more contraceptive teaching than ever before. In most states minors can receive birth control without parental notification. More and more teenagers are using contraceptives. According to Louis Harris and Associates in *American Teens Speak: Sex, Myths, TV, and Birth Control* (New York: Planned Parenthood Federation of America, 1986), p. 19, as many as 79 percent of all sexually active teens are using some form of birth control. And yet the number and rate of unmarried teen pregnancies keeps rising. Sis, teaching them about birth control and making it available to them is not reducing teen pregnancy—and for very good reasons! Let me list some of them:

Reason #1: Teens know intellectually that sex makes babies. But their thinking is often, "It [pregnancy] won't happen to me; I'm special" (the same kind of thinking that makes the sixteen-year-old drunk driver racing at one hundred miles per hour believe he won't get caught or have an accident). They think they are invulnerable.

Reason #2: Most teenagers just aren't responsible enough to take birth control consistently.

Reason #3: Teens know they live in a nuclear, "atom-bomb" world that could end tomorrow.

Reason #4: Some teenage pregnancies are intentional acts—conscious or subconscious. Girls have babies because they want to trap the father into marriage, to gain status with peers, to rebel against parents, or simply to have someone to love.

Reason #5: Studies show that many teens get pregnant within a year after a major family event: a death, divorce, mother going back to work, and so on. In other words, teenage pregnancy is often indicative of problematic family relationships that won't be solved by the quick fix of birth control.

Teens are growing out of childhood and into adulthood. Learning responsibility with new freedom is a constant challenge. And we adults aren't helping much when we send conflicting messages such as:

"Use your contraceptives; be grown up and responsible." BUT "It's illegal for a man to have intercourse with a girl under sixteen—she's just too young to be responsible."

"The pill is a potent hormone that blocks brain hormones and acts on young ovaries to interrupt regular menstrual periods. You can get it free without your parents' consent through a school-based clinic." BUT "You can't take an aspirin or get your ears pierced without parental permission."

"The VD rate is up; AIDS is rising to epidemic proportions; teen pregnancies, births, and abortions are up significantly." BUT "You can get three for free" (three free condoms given free).

"We know you can't control your sexual urges, so take this pill and have more sex with fewer problems." BUT "Just say no" to health hazards of alcohol, drugs, and cigarettes."

Sis, the list could go on. Adults can't give meaningful help to teenagers in this area because sexuality for adult Americans is out of control. Pornography, promiscuity, extramarital sex, homosexual and bisexual lifestyles abound. It's not surprising that adults are quick to put young people on birth control. They don't want to face up to more difficult issues such as:

teaching kids how—and why!—to say no to sex

acknowledging that the pill, the IUD, and RU-486 are used to cause early abortions. For example, when the pill isn't preventing conception, it changes the uterine lining to reject implantation of the fertilized egg.

modeling fidelity and self-control in married relationships

In so many families artificial birth control has replaced self-control with a false sense of security. So many people worry about getting pregnant. There is a real fear of children—especially unplanned children. Growing numbers of married couples are choosing to remain childless.

Sis, was it simpler in the days of trusting God as the One who knew when and how many babies? It's rare to meet parents of large families who say, "I wish I never had the last three or four children."

I read recently a comment on artificial birth control in marriage. Nordis Christenson, a Protestant pastor's wife, writes (*Christian Couple* [Minneapolis: Bethany House, 1977]):

Our actions speak more forcefully to our deep mind than do our intellectual rationalizations. Do we set up a conflict within ourselves when we attempt to say with one action, "I want to be one with you," while with another action we imply, "I reject the possible consequences of this oneness"? One intelligent, cultured, internationally traveled woman said to me, that she felt she had suffered

mental illness while taking the pill because of a schizo-
phrenic division of sexuality from personality (p. 75).

I know I started talking about birth control as a solution to the teenage pregnancy problem and have now
switched to the issue of artificial birth control for married couples. I believe they are two sides of the same coin.
I know there are some in the pro-life movement who feel
differently about birth control. But I think it would be
hard to disagree that self-esteem and self-control are
important qualities for us all.

Sis, thanks for listening.

14

Pointing Fingers

Dear Sis,

I find a rising anger in me at times as I look at the current state of affairs. In this war over abortion, the two camps are firmly pitted against each other. The pro-abortion activists prefer to be called "pro-choice." The pro-lifers would quickly retort "Pro-choice is *no* choice for the baby—only death." Name-calling, angry picket signs, demonstrations and arrests in front of each other's clinics or centers make the news almost weekly. The yearly March for Life was recently countered by the March for Abortion Rights. Ads appear regularly in papers, magazines, buses and billboards. Both sides claim to be advocates for the women and children involved. Each side prays for deliverance from their enemy. They pray for justice, truth, and peace to reign. It's truly a bloody war.

Within the pro-life camp there are many internal battle fronts as well. Some are committed to education and research, some to applying political lobbying pressure; some push legal reform, services for mothers and babies, adoption agencies, sidewalk counselors, maternity homes, operation rescue, postabortion counseling, and so on.

Each group fights the battle according to its priorities. Some pro-lifers pressure medical and mental-health professionals who perform, refer, or promote abortions. Some criticize apathetic Christian communities and churches for their ignorance on the subject of abortion and pastors for their unwillingness to lead their congregations against the evil. Still other pro-life groups speak out on the prevailing media bias against values. Media spokespeople rarely give equal time and opportunity to pro-life events or arguments. The problem is, each group seems to think its priorities are the only ones!

This bickering over practices and philosophies only serves to strip all the pro-life groups from their power source. When we start focusing on each other and the 10 percent we disagree on rather than marshalling forces on the 90 percent we jointly stand behind, our effectiveness fails.

Amid the myriad of causes and the confusion of the battlefront, Satan's strategy is clear:

Step 1: Let the 10-percent activists on either side of the argument remain angry, bitter, and resentful of the other side, so that they cancel each other out.

Step 2: Keep the majority—80 or so percent—apathetic, ignorant, complacent, and uninvolved in the issue.

Step 3: Breed dissension and disunity in the pro-life groups so they start attacking each other on their differences rather than focusing on their united agenda.

Result: Anger, bitterness, resentment, apathy, accusation equals—no spiritual power. Fingers pointing at each other shifts the focus off the real spiritual battle.

Sis, it looks like a well-planned strategy, but thank God that "greater is he [God] that is in us than he [Satan] who is in the world" (1 John 4:4, paraphrased). The Scriptures told us long ago in Zechariah 4 that victory comes "not by might, nor by power," but by the Lord's spirit (v. 6).

It's easy to see the problems, but how do we work toward the solutions? Everyone probably has his or her own agenda for action. The things that come to my mind are:

1. *We need to stop the negatives*—to cease condemning the enemy, judging fellow pro-lifers, and participating in gossip, backbiting, or criticism. We also need to ask forgiveness for wrongs inflicted.

2. *We need to ask God for humility.* Our pride surfaces so quickly. We forget that we are only "earthen vessels"—only God has the power. To use another analogy, we're the glove and he's the hand inside.

3. *We need to pray,* to tune in to God's heart for everyone involved. I've heard it said, "If we want to talk to people about God, we need first to talk to God about people." Only God holds the key to each human heart, and we must pray and pray and pray for God's will to be done in us and around us.

4. *We need to learn to love one another.* It's easier said than done. But it *can* be done if we put Jesus first in our lives, letting him so fill us with his unconditional love that we can be instruments of that love to all others.

Sis, I'm sure there's much more. Stopping the negatives, asking for humility, praying, loving one another are tall orders from a big God. I know a Christian OB nurse who has chosen to work in a Catholic hospital so she doesn't have to get involved in assisting in abortions. But she still ends up working labor and delivery with patients who have had previous abortions.

Until recently, if Kathy found a history of an abortion, her whole attitude would change; she would immediately battle very condemning thoughts toward that woman and her current need. Kathy admits she would judge these women as hardened, selfish killers who deserved serious complications in later pregnancies.

Upset to find the anger and hatred in her heart, Kathy asked God to forgive her. And then, Kathy told me, "the

Lord showed me a part of myself. My sin, my darkness is the same as theirs. All the sin that was ever committed existed in me. I am the woman who has had an abortion. I am the thief, the rapist, the murderer. I share in it all, and Jesus does, too. He suffers and carries our sin. I love the women you are ministering to and I pray for both of you."

Kathy's pointing fingers in this area has stopped and she now counsels and prays with women who come for help after their abortions. What a transformation God can make in a person's heart.

Pray for me that I can live what I believe, especially when the heat is on.

Thanks for listening.

15

Prevention

Dear Sis,

Day after day, frightened women enter our doors for pregnancy tests and support. The influx of needy people never seems to stop, and the numbers keep increasing. Of course, we pray that the Lord *will* increase the numbers—especially the number of abortion-minded women that we can serve. And we pray for more pregnancy centers to be established. The work of providing alternatives to abortion at the community grassroots level must continue. The need is so great. And if the abortion law were changed tomorrow, we would be hard pressed to handle all the needs with the current number of pregnancy centers available.

But, Sis, as important as this work is, it is only a part of what is needed. Problem pregnancies and abortions are the symptoms of much bigger illnesses in our society.

You know that before I entered this heated abortion arena I was an educator, counselor, and a medical professional. In it all, my heart has always been in wanting to prevent problems rather than just trying to solve them. In terms of my work now, this means preventing the need for young people to come to our center for any crisis.

We see girl after girl, woman after woman, who didn't want to "go all the way." Most of them were looking for love and affection and wanting to be held close to someone. We often hear the excuse, "He's so interested in doing it." Then she says yes to intercourse to get that physical closeness and he says yes to holding her to get intercourse.

I'm not ignoring the times girls push guys for sex. But more often than not, the women we see were happy with just being held.

Often we'll ask, "Have you thought about saying no when he wants to go to bed with you?"

And here are some of the answers we hear:

A laugh!

"No, I guess I haven't thought about it."

"He says he can't stop once he gets going."

"I don't know what he'd do."

"I don't know how to say no."

It's the last answer that really saddens me. Sis, where are the adults to teach young people like this how to say no and why? Where are the parents, teachers, youth leaders, pastors, and caring older adults whose voices will counteract the voices of the media, the peer group, the pill-pushing school-based clinic, and so on? Where are the adults who will dedicate themselves to being the role models of fidelity in relationships to God, spouse, children, church, and neighborhood?

Words about chastity must be backed up by lives that bear the fruit of godly relationships. Kids quickly spot hypocrites who don't practice what they preach. Young people are searching for truth—for good ideals to strive for and dreams to challenge all their gifts and talents.

The adults who believe in chastity and are living faithful lives have a message to share. Kids are hungry for true goodness and a life of commitment that is holy and right. Young people want to be stretched to grow toward important values.

Who will believe in our young people enough to help them learn that:

God's laws are best. Our creator is a master psychologist who knows that sex outside of marriage will harm us.

Self-control in the area of sexuality is possible, desirable and a great freedom to be sought.

How to say no in the tough situations is a skill that can be learned once we have sorted out our values.

It pays to serve God. Striving for God's best in our lives is infinitely worth it.

Sis, it's so easy for me to get carried away on this topic. I recently heard a speaker mention that when "God shows you a problem it's because you're going to be part of the solution." Pray that I listen to the Holy Spirit to know and do my part in this solution.

Thanks again for listening.

16

A Temple

Dear Sis,

At a recent conference luncheon I sat with an instructor from a nearby university medical school. She told me about something that occurred recently when the anti-abortion film, *Silent Scream*, was shown in one of the school's ethics classes. The students were offended by Dr. Bernard Nathanson's use of words. In the beginning of the film the clinical term *uterus* is employed to refer to the woman's primary reproductive organ. Then Dr. Nathanson uses the less scientific word *womb*, followed by *tomb* at the end of the film.

For the scientifically minded medical students, this sequence of terminology was infuriating. They were so incensed by the language that they couldn't or wouldn't tune in to the message.

How grateful I was for the chance to hear this story. It reminded me to be careful and to know my audience—Jesus would say, to be "wise as serpents and innocent as doves" (Matt. 10:16 RSV). Whether I am speaking to parents, young people, health professionals, clergy, or educators—I must present the truth to each group in language they can understand. Jesus was a great example. He talked to fisherman about storms and fish. He talked to farmers about seeds, vines, and fruit. He talked to shepherds about sheep, goats, and wolves. Surely he would talk to medical students in medical terms!

But when I think about "uterus-womb-tomb," the word that follows in my mind is *temple*. That small pear-shaped organ in every woman has the potential to become a holy house, a special temple of God for the nine months of pregnancy. At conception God breathes his eternal, abundant life into that new being. That tiny, developing preborn child who will live forever reflects an image of God that will never be duplicated. The preborn is a temple, a house of God within a growing "room," the womb of his or her mother.

Sis, when I watch videos on fetal life, I often hear in my head the words of the song, "In this very room . . . Jesus is in this very room." Isn't it amazing that the great God of all creation would choose to take up residence inside each of us at the time of our conception!

Sis, have I mentioned a few facts about the incredibly special way each human being begins?

At twelve weeks after conception the female preborn has four hundred thousand eggs stored in her tiny ovaries. At puberty, one egg is released each month.

The male at intercourse releases up to a half-billion—yes, five hundred million sperm swimming to find one egg—the egg of the month.

Of the thousands of sperm that swarm around the egg, one and only one penetrates. That moment of fertilization or conception is a microscopic explosion of God's life. Human life begins.

Carlo Caretto states it well: "Human life is born at conception and never ends even if death occurs in the first months, making a tomb of the mother's womb" (*Journey Without End* [Notre Dame, IN.: Ave Maria Press, 1989], p. 7). He stresses that we are eternal because

God is eternal. From the time we are conceived in our mother's body, we are unique. Never will the same egg and sperm, each with its own particular genetic code, meet again.

For a while mom's womb is a temple to house this holy act of God. Her body is the shell that surrounds the eternal life of a spirit and soul that will live forever.

Sis, this subject gets so involved. Pregnancy is a mystery. Scientists and physicians don't know the answers to why pregnancy is two hundred eighty days, what starts labor pains, or many other questions surrounding the miracle of life.

The spiritual realities of eternal life beginning at conception and each of us having our own guardian angel to care for us—well, it "blows my circuits" at times. It makes me wonder why we were created. I feel it's connected to worship, being in relationship with the one who created us.

Lord, teach us about being temples, caring for our temples, being builders of preborn temples, about being people of worship every day.

Sis, I know I've been rambling on. I'm grateful for the unique, divinely created person you are.

Thanks for listening.

Three

Mourning:
A Baby Dies

17

Miscarriage

Dear Sis,

In my part of the country, spring is a beautiful time of the year, a time of picnics and lots of outdoor activities. All of nature shouts with vibrant life! Yet even in the midst of this time of celebration, I am thinking of two young women who have recently come through our pregnancy center.

The first woman—I'll call her Janet—was on her way to have an abortion when a friend talked her into coming to meet with us. She really didn't want to have an abortion, but she couldn't see any other way at the time. She admitted to us that she wanted to be talked out of going ahead with the abortion.

She was alone and frightened, with a long history of being rejected. Sharing her story and finding people who cared and could walk through this pregnancy with her, made the difference in her choosing not to abort that baby within her womb.

Our prayers that she would find the courage to tell her family were answered with a miracle! Profound healing between Janet and her family took place because of the presence of that sacred life within her. Medical care, job details, family support—all fell into place as preparations continued.

And then a follow-up phone call revealed that Janet had miscarried.

First to be so close to aborting, then to be so excited about the new life within her, now so empty . . . what an emotional roller coaster! Janet didn't want to talk with us about the miscarriage; her feelings ran too deep.

Marcia is the other young woman who is on my heart these days. Marcia denied for a long time the possibility of her being pregnant. She kept making excuses for morning sickness and other symptoms of pregnancy. Then she seriously considered abortion, put off medical care, tried to act as if nothing was happening.

Together we worked through Marcia's fears of a first pelvic exam, of facing her co-workers, of her future. Marcia's parents and the father of the baby would not be involved. What a burden to carry—so far from home and supporting herself. Marcia's history of sexual abuse when she was a child made the problems even more complicated.

The doctor warned her of possible medical problems stemming from sexual abuse she had suffered as a child. Marcia knew she should avoid heavy lifting in the months ahead.

One day Marcia called to describe some symptoms she was having. They didn't sound good. Yes, she had lifted heavy boxes. She put off the call to the doctor.

And next I was hearing that Marcia had miscarried at home and driven herself to the emergency room. What emptiness she described!

This is the season of Marcia's due date—a tough time emotionally. In the safe walls of the pregnancy center she painfully verbalized her haunting questions:

"Was my baby a boy or a girl?"

"What color were his or her eyes and hair?"

"Who would he or she have looked like?"

"If I hadn't lifted those boxes, would my baby be alive today?"

"What kind of mother would I have been?"

"Did my baby feel pain?"

"Would my baby have loved me?"

"Is God punishing me?"

"Did I really want my baby to live? . . ."

Chances are that Janet has faced or will face some of the same thoughts. In sharing with many women who have had miscarriages, abortions and stillbirths, I have found the similarities striking. Each mother who suffers one of these three sad events has to grieve the death of her preborn child and to deal with no longer being pregnant.

Each mother's process of grieving is unique and personal. Emotions can range from anger, guilt (real or imagined), depression, relief, remorse, fear, joy, isolation, or emptiness. Her spiritual concepts of God, church, heaven, hell, and prayer will all be challenged. Her body will undergo drastic physical changes to return to a nonpregnant state after gearing up for labor, delivery, and nursing.

Meanwhile, those around her—family, friends, and co-workers—may either:

encourage her to grieve,

deny that grieving is necessary, or

just say nothing and disappear (probably because they feel awkward).

Grieving for miscarried children is real. Allowing moms, dads, and families to work through that death and loss is a great gift. After all, those children are as real as you and I. In fact, Scripture tells us that God has called each of us by name before we were born!

Sis, thanks again for listening.

18

Grief

Dear Sis,

Working with women in crisis pregnancies challenges me to grow in so many areas of my life. A while ago, I wrote about sensing the little one inside the womb, cheering me on in loving his or her mom. In another letter, I told you how angry I get with moms who force their daughters to have abortions.

Now I realize once again that, except for God's grace in my life, I could easily be doing the same. Sis, my emotions get stretched in so many different directions. Today I need to tell you about something that happened recently.

I was out of state visiting my friend Jane, who was about to speak at a women's Bible study. Before the talk began, seven women sat at a table getting to know each other. When they discovered I work with women in crisis pregnancies, the conversation switched to asking me lots of questions.

I shared about the day-to-day work with women. And I explained some of the patterns we see in the center:

Women who are so frightened by the thought of an unplanned pregnancy that they become emotionally paralyzed.

Women for whom the problem pregnancy is just a symptom of bigger, unresolved problems of years past; often child abuse, alcoholic families, divorce, etc.

Women who abort and then get pregnant again within the year or so afterward, despite their insistence on using the best birth control possible.

As the conversation ended, we rose to hear Jane. Sarah, who had been sitting at the table, touched my arm and said, "I was one of those women you just described. Twenty-two years ago I got pregnant at seventeen, panicked, and decided abortion was the only way out. I had caused lots of problems at home. A pregnancy out of wedlock would have been the straw that broke the camel's back.

"Well, within the year after the abortion, I was pregnant again and not married. I knew I could not abort this baby. I had my son and two weeks later married someone not the father.

"Life was rocky for a long time. Though I had given my life to Christ as a young teenager, most of those years I wasn't following Him.

"Five years ago I was so unhappy I gave up trying to put my life together. I had already asked Jesus Christ into my heart. I had asked him to forgive me for the abortion and all the sins of my life. I had been attending church and learning that I was a new creature in Christ. For two years my faith grew, and I could honestly repeat the words, 'I am forgiven by the blood of the Lamb shed for me.' But I still wasn't free. Thinking about the abortion really brought me down.

"Then my pastor's wife said to me, 'Sarah, you've never buried that child!' I knew she was right, and I knew I had to do something. I prayed God would show me what it was.

"I took some wood and made a little white cross with Diana's name on it. (I had sensed the baby was a girl and had named her Diana.) I ran up to the top of a mountain a few miles from home and I planted that cross in the ground. Then I sat on a rock and cried all day. And I knew God was there with me as I mourned for my little girl."

I could see in Sarah's wet eyes the intense pain of that experience—yet her joy in knowing that her aborted child had been released to God's care was just as intense. She could now talk of knowing God's forgiveness to the depths of her being. She shared how she had been able to forgive herself since that day.

Sis, I wonder why I didn't have to learn of God's forgiving love the way Sarah did. And I wonder about those who have never allowed themselves to grieve for their aborted child. It's so humbling and awesome to watch God's healing touch in the lives of his precious ones.

Thanks for listening.

19

Postabortion

Dear Sis,

For years I have had an intense desire to learn about helping those who have suffered abortions, miscarriages, and stillbirths. I don't know why, but the urgency is real. Recently in the media the debate regarding the psychological ill effects of abortion has heightened. Attending workshops and reading extensively on the topic of postabortion syndrome has confirmed what I've learned from women and men in the counseling room. Though someone can have these symptoms because of an abortion, there may be factors prior to the abortion that are crucial in discerning the source of problems.

Sis, bear with me as I'm preparing a talk on postabortion syndrome and need to get my thoughts together.

I like the way Teri and Paul Reisser in their book *Help for the Post-Abortion Woman* (Grand Rapids, MI.: Zondervan Publishing House, 1989) list the symptoms of postabortion syndrome:

guilt
anxiety
psychological numbing
depression and thoughts of suicide

sad mood

sudden and uncontrollable crying episodes

deterioration of self-concept

sleep, appetite, and sexual disturbances

reduced motivation

disruption of interpersonal relationships

thoughts of suicide

anniversary syndrome

reexperiencing the abortion

preoccupation with becoming pregnant again

anxiety over fertility and childbearing issues

disruption of the bonding process with present and/or
future children

survival guilt

development of eating disorders

alcohol and drug abuse

other self-punishing or self-degrading behaviors

brief reactive psychosis

The Reissers spend pages explaining each of these. They also add the statement that if someone has recently experienced three or more symptoms in relation to an abortion the likelihood is the person is suffering from postabortion syndrome.

Sis, the studies surrounding postabortion stress reveal data that can be important in counseling women before they decide to abort or not to abort, as well as for those who have already aborted. Postabortion stress will be more severe if the following conditions exist.

The Predisposition factors:

a maternal orientation,

prior children,

prior abortions,

religious affiliation and/or conservatism,

a lack of relationship support,

force or coercion,

more advanced pregnancy,

genetic abortion (as opposed to one for elective reasons),

preabortion ambivalence,

history of emotional problems,

low self-esteem,

lack of support in family of origin,

adolescence (teen pregnancy)

As I look at this list, I think of B. J. She first came to our center for a pregnancy test. At first she was excited when it turned out positive; the relationship with the father was a problem, but she figured she could raise her baby on her own. B. J. worked at a nursing home and had a great love for old folks, young kids, and everyone in between. She's what we would call a "big heart client."

B. J. left the center intending to carry her baby to term. But when the volunteer called to follow up and see how B. J. was doing, she learned that B. J. had aborted her baby. She had been in an automobile accident, and the X-ray technician had forgotten to ask about possible pregnancy. When the doctors discovered she had had a bunch of X-rays, they said, "Your baby will be deformed; you must have an abortion." She had believed them and scheduled the procedure.

Six months later, B. J. appeared at the doors of the pregnancy center again. She looked awful. The tears wouldn't stop, and she kept repeating, "I must talk to somebody."

Sis, it was the expected due date of her aborted baby, and "anniversary syndrome" had hit hard for B. J. She was hurting all over—she couldn't eat right, sleep well, or concentrate at work, and she had been acting crazy in her relationships. She was so withdrawn and quiet that I even wondered about suicide plans.

B. J. assured me she was not thinking suicide, but she knew she needed help, so we set her up a schedule for postabortion counseling. Over the course of her subsequent visits, it was wonderful to watch the healing process take place in this sensitive daughter of God who was aware of her need and open to receiving God's grace.

In the second postabortion visit, I asked B. J. if she had a sense as to whether her child was a boy or a girl. She quickly responded, "It was a girl and I named her Diedre Marie. In fact, I took my baptismal certificate from church and erased my name, inserted Diedre Marie, and dedicated my little girl to God. I believe Jesus is raising my child in heaven."

Sis, there was absolute conviction in her voice. I was awed at how much God had already done in healing this woman. B. J. had asked God's forgiveness early on. She was now struggling to forgive her boyfriend and the doctor whose statement about "possible deformities" had convinced her to abort.

As we explored that issue, I remember asking B. J. what she would have done if her baby had been born with a handicap. She answered, "I would have loved her even more than usual." B. J. knew she had a lot of love to give. Her maternal orientation, the pressure from the doctors, her lack of family and relationship support, and her deep religious beliefs all set her up to suffer more because of her abortion decision. But she was ready to put that suffering behind her and keep on reaching out to love and be loved.

B. J. was one of the fortunate ones. In her subsequent sessions she worked through her grief and asked forgiveness from God, her Baptist pastor, her baby, and even herself.

Sometimes I wonder how many lives have been touched by abortion—directly or indirectly. If every

mother, father, grandparent, sibling, of an aborted baby—
as well as everyone who has performed an abortion,
assisted with or encouraged one, or made a living in any
way connected to the abortion industry—had a giant "A"
on their chest as they walked around, the numbers would
be beyond belief.

I'm sure there is a greater percentage of women sitting
in church pews who have had abortions than the percentage of postabortive women in the general population. So
often the abortion experience is what drives a woman to
recognize her need for Jesus as Savior and Lord of her life.

Jesus, thank you that we can come to you in our sin.
Lord, you have paid the price for all of our sins to be
forgiven—even the sin of abortion. In your great mercy
forgive us Lord. Let us experience the cleansing gift of
forgiveness. Heal each of us in the areas we need it most.
Jesus teach us how to love you more and to receive all the
love and mercy you desire to bestow.

Sis, we have so much to learn about the aftereffects of
abortion. Only those who have had abortions can teach
us about the experience. Pray that we learn quickly—
and help.

Thanks for listening.

20

For Dads

Dear Sis,

This pregnancy-center business is lopsided. We see many more women in crisis than men. Yet I've come to believe there are many hurting men who never talk about, cry over, and mourn their aborted child.

My first encounter with a father grieving the death of his aborted daughter came in a TV studio—on the air. Late one night I had received a call from a stranger. He was looking for a Christian who knew something about abortion to drive forty miles and sit in the audience of a local TV talk show early the next morning. Why not? So I asked a friend to join me and arrived at the station, not knowing what to expect.

The program host introduced Jeff, a good-looking twenty-one-year-old college student. Jeff and his girlfriend, Jackie, had been dating a while when she became pregnant. Jackie decided to have an abortion. And even though Jeff was really against the abortion, he was unable to persuade her not to have it. So Jeff had accompanied Jackie to the abortion clinic for what he described as "the most miserable day in my life." As his story unfolded, Jeff's heart was breaking right in front of us and the whole TV audience. We could see his great remorse and anguish as he blurted out, "My daughter would have been one month old today."

The next guest on the program was a counselor from a local college who helped men after abortions. He offered standard listening skills and some suggestions for men in their perceived time of crisis. But his insights didn't seem to be helping Jeff much.

All this time I kept praying silently for Jeff and for those in the studio. And I prayed to know what God wanted me to do. Jeff had mentioned he was raised in a Christian home, and I felt I had to say something to point this hurting young man to Jesus, the healer of all life.

Because the TV talk show took comments from the audience, I asked to use the microphone. At first I was refused permission, so I waited and then tried again. When I got the signal to start, I looked straight at Jeff and explained that people grieving the loss of their aborted child have found certain things helpful during the mourning process. Jeff's Christian background and his belief that the preborn child is a human person made it easier to explain. Jeff already knew the sex of the child; the doctor had told him it was a girl. So I told Jeff he could name his daughter (God calls each of us by name before we were born) and have a memorial service for the child.

The host interrupted and said, "Wait a minute; you're acting like this is a baby that died a few days after birth— and you're having a funeral service for the dead child."

"That's right." I explained, "For Jeff, the father, it is a real child. Jeff's daughter is very real to him." The host quickly turned to Jeff and asked, "What do you think about that?"

Jeff's eyes glistened with hope as he said, "I never thought I could do that." He was visibly helped in that two- minute encounter. What a relief and a victory!

The producer of the program approached me at the end of the show to thank me for my comments. She explained that they had no idea Jeff had not worked through the abortion experience. They would have never put him on the air if they had known he was hurting so badly. "You gave him permission to grieve and mourn the loss of his daughter."

The experience with Jeff and other fathers whose children have been aborted prepared me for the day I went to speak on a local radio station about postabortion counseling. This was a call-in talk show, and Pete called soon after the break.

Pete, a twenty-six-year-old businessman, recounted the story of his girlfriend's abortion seven years before. He described how he hadn't really liked the idea of abortion but hadn't asserted his opinions with his girlfriend. Then, after the abortion, the reality hit him. He tried to function as if nothing had happened, but it didn't work. Pete couldn't pay attention in his college classes, couldn't concentrate on his tests, couldn't do anything. Eventually he dropped out of school. He tried to talk to his girlfriend about the abortion, but she was too enmeshed in her own world of denial and numbness. Finally Pete broke down. He was hospitalized for several weeks to get his head and heart to work together. Pete admitted that his healing over these past six years has been a long, slow process, but Jesus has helped him every step of the way.

Part of Pete's great remorse was that the pregnancy and abortion happened soon after he had committed his life to the lordship of Jesus. He had thought he was stronger and could resist the physical temptations. Today, Pete firmly declares that he knows both his own weakness and the tremendous power of God in the midst of his trials. Pete shared so much on that broadcast that all of us were amazed. Soon afterward he made an appointment at our center for postabortion counseling.

Jeff and Pete are two of many, many dads who mourn—and who will mourn in days ahead:

Dads who didn't want their child aborted—or maybe wanted it at the time and changed their minds;

Dads who are sorry they paid for the abortion;

Dads who regret going with the mom to the clinic;

Dads who are angry at their sense of powerlessness to stop the abortion;

Dads who were ambivalent or wishy-washy at the time their wives or girlfriends needed them to be strong and decisive;

Dads who fall apart when they think of what could have been;

Dads who are supposed to keep their feelings in and move forward, but just cannot forget . . .

Father God, you who teach us what fatherhood is all about, help us now. Little boys and little girls have died, and their dads don't know where to turn. Help them to know, understand, and receive your forgiving mercy. They don't know how to mourn and grieve for their lost child or children. You lost your only Son, Jesus, to a violent, bloody death on a cross. Console these dads who mourn. Cradle them in your tender arms. Comfort them as only you can. Grant them the gift of tears, that they may express their grief and be able to see this experience through your eyes. And draw them close to you this day and always. It's in the precious name of Jesus we pray. Amen.

Sis, thanks again for listening.

21

For Grandparents

Dear Sis,

It's amazing how many lives are affected by an abortion. I need to tell you a story that left a profound impression on me.

One day Jason, a tall, distinguished, middle-aged gentlemen, appeared at the pregnancy center. It was awkward to see him come in and not know what to do with himself. As we settled down to talk, he quickly admitted that his teenaged daughter, Tracy, was pregnant—about four months along. His wife was out of town for an extended period of time, and the boyfriend/father of the baby was not involved, so granddad was handling these major decisions for his pregnant daughter.

Tracy, at thirteen, saw nothing wrong with recreational sex, nor had she considered the possibility that pregnancy could result from sexual intercourse. She was bright, articulate, and popular. Her main concern was that at sixteen weeks of pregnancy she couldn't fit into her cheerleading outfit.

Jason, who knew his daughter's maturity level, made arrangements for her medical care and subsequent placement in a group home for unwed teen mothers. Tracy was amenable, and trusted her dad. After the ultrasound had been done to confirm the baby's size and due dates, I sensed Jason's relief that Tracy was doing fine. There were numbers of phone calls and visits in the following days.

One day I called and Tracy answered. I told her I was calling to say hi and see how she was doing. Very matter-of-factly she stated, "I had my abortion yesterday. I stayed home from school today, but I'm fine. Dad took me."

I was dumbfounded. A few weeks ago, I had sat with Jason and heard him say, "I don't want my daughter to have an abortion" and "I'm excited the details at the maternity home have worked out so well." Now, I was hearing he had arranged an abortion at the only hospital in that area that would abort so late in the pregnancy.

Sis, I don't know if Jason is openly mourning the loss of his granddaughter—the ultrasound showed a girl. I know I mourned that child's death more than most. Someday, Jason may regret what has happened. Meanwhile, the family needs our prayers.

Another story comes to mind when I think of grandparents and abortion. Recently I was speaking to volunteers at another pregnancy center on postabortion trauma. I mentioned that the grandparents, brothers and sisters or other family members involved can experience postabortion syndrome. In the middle of my sentence, a woman from the back of the room started relating what happened more than ten years ago when her seventeen-year-old daughter aborted a child, Ann's first grandchild. Ann said she had been so distraught at the news she had to be hospitalized in the psychiatric unit for over a week with emotional problems she didn't understand.

As I described the cluster of symptoms that can occur after an abortion, she recognized her need to mourn and work through the loss of her grandchild. Fortunately, Ann knew the comfort of Jesus in her time of sorrow.

Sis, I wonder how many parents—grandparents, really— grieve over discovering the abortion plans too late. I've heard their heartache over the fact that their son or daughter was too afraid to come home to them with the crisis pregnancy. This was one point in their lives when they needed the love and support of their parents yet the child went elsewhere.

I'm reminded of Proverbs 17: "Children's children are a crown to the aged" (v. 6). Whenever there is an abortion, a grandparent is deprived of that crown.

Dear Father, you are a family God. You understand losing loved ones. Comfort the grieving grandparents who are unable to touch, see, and love their grandchild. Enable them to receive the love and consolation that only you can give. For families who don't know if a child has been aborted, touch them with your love and mercy. Heal the broken families of today.

Thanks, Lord.

Sis, thanks for listening.

22

For Doctors and Nurses

Dear Sis,

Soon after I started working at the crisis pregnancy center, Dr. Tom arrived unannounced at my office and told me his story. In his early years of practice as a new, ambitious obstetrician/gynecologist, he performed many, many abortions. Later, he gave his life to Jesus, and major areas of his life changed. His conscience got the better of him, and he knew he had to cease the abortions. When I met him, it had been over a year since his last abortion and he had vowed never to start again. I commended Dr. Tom on his decision to do what he knew God was asking.

As our conversation continued, the question of "referrals for abortion" arose. His reply was, "I wouldn't refer any of your patients for an abortion." I asked if he referred any patients. He answered, "Yes, but only a few." I was stunned, and he was surprised to see my shock and disbelief. At that moment he truly saw no problem with referring for abortions. "After all, there are a lot of bad butchers out there."

I was quietly praying for wisdom, sensing God was about to do something. I asked Dr. Tom, "What if a patient comes into my office, explains he is planning to kill his brother-in-law next week, and asks me to present

99

the different means available—or even suggest a hit man
for the job? Do I comply? Or what if a patient wants to
commit suicide and asks my help in recommending the
most lethal and least painful techniques of taking one's
own life? Do I give him what he wants just because he's
asking and I know some pertinent information?"

Dr. Tom's eyes opened wide—the connection was
made. And the change in his position was startling: "I
won't take a human life. I guess that means I can't refer
my patients to another doctor who will perform the
abortion, either. So I won't do it. I will not be an accom-
plice to the crime."

I brought up a related issue. "Dr. Tom, do you insert
IUDs (intrauterine devices)?

"Only a few," he answered.

"Does the IUD prevent conception?" Immediately he
knew my point. IUDs prevent implantation of the fertilized egg after conception has already occurred. Thus the
IUD is an early abortion method, not a contraceptive (a
device to keep conception from occurring). "I won't
insert IUDs, either" Tom said emphatically.

Dr. Tom and I prayed together before he left. It was a
poignant meeting. Step by step, God had used me to
reveal Tom's areas of blindness. He was truly sorry and
determined to live out his commitment.

Dr. Tom now works with several crisis pregnancy
centers in the area. He has made great sacrifices to care
for women and their families in their time of need. His
sorrow for the many abortions he performed is real.

Sis, participating in abortions can sneak up on a doctor
or nurse so easily. You know Betty, my nurse friend who
works at a local hospital. Betty, who works different
floors, recently told me the story of the night she was
distributing medications. Betty was supposed to give a
prostaglandin suppository (a hormone treatment) to a
woman on her wing. At first she thought nothing of
it; giving hormones to a woman patient is not that

uncommon. Then something clicked in Betty's mind—a prostaglandin suppository is a late abortion method. She decided to check why the patient was hospitalized. And listed in the orders she read, "pregnancy termination—second trimester."

Betty had to go to her supervisor to inform her that she would not administer the drug. The supervisor herself administered the suppository. And Betty took a break, went to the restroom, and cried—tears for what she almost did, tears for the mother and baby, tears for the supervisor and hospital.

Ever since that night, Betty has been struggling with whether or not to change jobs. Working so close to abortions is taking its toll on her.

Sis, there are many doctors and nurses caught in a profession that promotes abortions without batting a eye. But the number of those who will not perform abortions, help with them, or refer for them is slowly growing. Helping them come to this point requires loving them one by one, just as we love the women in crisis who walk through our doors.

Sis, pray with me, please.

Father, please send your Holy Spirit to open the eyes and hearts of your people to the evil of abortion. Show us our blindness, and give us your forgiveness for the ways we have contributed to the problems before us. Show us how to pray for our fellow wounded healers who are doctors and nurses. Cleanse and restore the healing professions to their original purpose of assisting you, the divine Physician and the Healer of all life. Lord, thank you for your faithfulness even when we are unfaithful.

Thanks for listening.

23

For Counselors, Teachers, and Friends

Dear Sis,

I've mentioned before that this job doesn't end when I close the door of the pregnancy center. It's as if God makes me a magnet for those who need to talk about their pregnancy-related crisis.

I was attending a conference and renewing my old friendship with Gerry, who is a marriage and family therapist, when she stopped in mid-conversation to announce, "Ellen, I need to tell you something." Her tone of voice was serious, and fortunately we were in a place where we could talk.

Gerry told me, "A few weeks ago my friend Suzanne called me at 7:15 A.M. to say she was scheduled for an abortion later that morning. So I put on my 'clinical hat,' and did what I was trained to do as a counselor. I listened. I remained neutral and withheld my true feelings, even though I felt awkward and really torn. Suzanne did have her abortion that day. I'm not sure how she's doing, but I have felt awful about the whole thing since that morning. I did what I was supposed to do, but I can't shake the feeling that I missed something."

Sis, I weep both for Suzanne and her baby. Yet I'm glad Gerry is disturbed—she's really hungry to learn from this encounter.

I explained to Gerry that she missed Suzanne's cry for help. Suzanne knew Gerry's personal opinion about abortion. Her call a couple hours before the abortion showed her preabortion ambivalence, which is very common. Suzanne was undecided about her choice. She wanted Gerry to talk her out of the abortion and support her in her time of need.

Deep down, no woman really wants an abortion. Little girls don't grow up dreaming about their first abortion. Most women who opt for abortion do so because it seems to be the convenient way out of a very inconvenient pregnancy, not because it's what they really want. Many women experience "relief" immediately after the abortion, but not the "peace" for which they yearn.

Gerry thought she was doing well as a counselor, but she now admits she failed Suzanne as a counselor and a friend. Suzanne needed more than a listening ear. She needed to know about fetal development, abortion procedures, and the increased emotional risks for a woman in her early forties who already has children. She needed someone to tell her the truth and support her in making an informed decision.

I encouraged Gerry to seek out her local crisis pregnancy center and go through the training they offer. That way she will learn how to care for a woman in crisis, how to educate with accurate information on fetal development, abortion procedures, risks, and complications—physical, emotional, spiritual. Exploring the options of single parenting, adoption, or marriage with individuals who may have a minimal support system is a learnable skill.

Gerry, like most good counselors and teachers, is a good nurturer. She loves to watch people grow. Her gifts often enable others to move from darkness to light, from confusion to clarity, from fear of the future to a fullness of life. But when it comes to life-or-death issues, her responsibility doesn't end there. After all, a good counselor, teacher, or friend would never allow another to pursue suicidal or homicidal plans unchallenged. And abortion, too, is a life-or-death struggle.

Sis, I'm reminded of a popular high school teacher, Mrs. Smith, who often had students approach her after school for help. This teacher loved young people and the students trusted her, even though she challenged them often. I watched this teacher help students make arrangements for abortions, student after student. The word was out—this teacher would help. But the teacher finally drew the line after counseling one male senior and helping him arrange his girlfriend's third abortion.

Later Mrs. Smith admitted, "It was so easy to get sucked into helping these teens in crisis. I just didn't consider that my involvement in their abortion plans compromised my own position on abortion. But I just can't do it anymore."

Sis, Gerry and Mrs. Smith are two women who looked at their own values and thought through the abortion issue for themselves and for the clients and students they served. Please pray for them now with me.

Dear Lord, and Creator of all life, we need you in every area of our lives. Often we intend to do the right thing, but issues get confused so easily. Help Gerry and Mrs. Smith and all those like them who now struggle with bad decisions of the past. For the lives that have been lost, for the parents and others involved, we beg your mercy and forgiveness. Comfort, as only you can, those who mourn. Lord, please direct our paths.

Thanks Lord. And thanks, Sis, for listening.

24

For Ministers

Dear Sis,

Many kinds of people visit our pregnancy center, and God often surprises us with who he brings through the doors. One afternoon Father Jack, a local priest, visited and had time to chat. This man of God is widely recognized in our community, and he has a lot of experience in pro-life work.

Father Jack and I talked about many aspects of pro-life work in our geographic area as well as around the world. After two hours of sharing, he asked in a very serious tone, "What do you think has left the greatest impression on me from our conversation just now?" I ventured a guess and he shook his head no, then quickly told me the answer: "It was your story of the woman who had sought help and healing from three pastors, and each of them heaped more guilt on her as she confessed her abortion. You really need good ministers as referrals for women and men who are hurting after an abortion!"

I agreed and asked him to help me find competent, compassionate ministers who are educated on abortion and who know how to care for the other victims of abortion. Father Jack and I have been working together ever since that day.

Sis, in different parts of the country there are excellent outreach programs for women and men who are suffering after an abortion. Project Rachel is one of them. Sponsored by the Catholic church, this program equips priests and professional counselors to recognize the symptoms of postabortion trauma and to treat the sufferers spiritually, psychologically, and emotionally. Besides providing individual appointments for the sacraments of reconciliation or for counseling, Project Rachel offers healing services for anyone who has lost a child through abortion, miscarriage, or stillbirth.

I've met Baptist, Methodist, Presbyterian, Lutheran, and Pentecostal ministers who also have a heart both for helping women in crisis pregnancies and caring for the needs of those who suffer after abortions. Little by little, God is bringing men and women of God out of the woodwork to help in this area.

Sis, I've noticed that when a minister who has been inactive or silent in the abortion/pro-life controversy comes to a sanctity-of-life position an amazing change usually occurs. Godly sorrow for not getting involved sooner is often followed by a boldness and courage to speak out in defense of the preborn and their mothers caught in crisis pregnancies. The more aware and informed the minister becomes on the ramifications of abortion, the more his or her creative energies are engaged to find ways to help.

Once the minister takes a public stand, there may be church members who disagree with him or her. Some may even criticize the minister. But in my experience, congregations seem to understand that this man or woman of God is preaching against the sin of abortion, yet loving the sinner. The combination of actively working to stop the evil while extending the mercy and love of God to those in need provides a powerful model for the flock.

When pastors are willing to get arrested to save the lives of preborn children and the heartache of pregnant moms, people notice. I recently heard a bishop who had been arrested in an area-wide Operation Rescue remark that he was following the way of three greats before him—Jesus, Peter, and Paul were all arrested for the sake of the gospel. What an example to follow!

Sis, I think of Father Jack's sadness—the sadness of the other ministers I've seen weep over this abortion holocaust. Please pray with me now for them:

Dear Father in heaven, you know our hearts even before we open our mouths. Teach us how to pray. The men and women who are your ministers need a special anointing, a special touch of your Holy Spirit to lead your people. Empower your shepherds to lead the way in repentance, forgiveness, weeping, and mourning for abortions. Enable the shepherds to inspire their people to prayer and action, so the church will take its rightful place as the body of Christ on this earth. Lord, we all need you desperately. It's not by our might, nor by our power, but only by your Holy Spirit, (Zech. 4:6) that this can happen. Lord, we thank you in advance for the answer to our prayer.

Sis, thanks for your prayers, and thanks for listening.

Part Four
On a Mission

25

Ambassadors

Dear Sis,

An interesting thing has been happening to me since I started working at the pregnancy center.

Certain neighbors, friends, family, and fellow church members will approach me and ask, "How's it going at the pregnancy center?" They aren't just being polite; I sense their genuine interest. (The people who have referred clients to us in the past often feel they have a stake in our work.) Then, as I begin sharing details on how God is working in the lives of all of us connected to the center, many will open up about experiences from their past: a crisis pregnancy they or their child experienced, an abortion or adoption that happened years ago.

It's as if people gravitate toward me to share their stories of pregnancy-related events. I guess they sense it's OK to talk to me about these issues in their lives.

It is truly a gift to have either strangers or family members deem you worthy to know about intimate areas of their lives—a gift and a responsibility!

I keep thinking of something I read in Michael Mannion's book, *Abortion and Healing: A Cry to Be Whole* (Kansas City, MO.: Sheed and Ward). In speaking of helping a woman after an abortion, he quotes Father

Vincent Dwyer: "A holy person is one in whose presence I feel sacred about myself. The more comfortable, trusting, and open she becomes with you, the deeper the friendship. A positive friendship is transformed into spiritual intimacy when she is led to look beyond you and see the person of Christ in you, when she sees God seeing her as you see her, when the sacredness she feels she possesses in God's eyes is reflected in the sacredness she feels in your eyes" (p. 71).

Sis, I pray that others will feel sacred about themselves in my presence. I want them to know they are accepted and loved just as they are—by me, and especially by the God who created them, who is reaching from heaven toward them. I also pray that people will look at me and see the love of Jesus shining out of my eyes.

I think of the special people God has sent in my life to pick me up when I sinned. The brothers and sisters who told me about and showed me that unconditional love I needed so desperately. For me, the experience of being able to share my intimate, ugly self with others and still be accepted was life-changing! Truly, I am who I am today because of those who have loved me.

You and mom and dad were the first people to show me that kind of love. How can I thank you? But our family love was just a tiny foretaste of God's love to me. He says, "Before I formed you in the womb, I knew you" (Jer. 1:5). He's loved me totally since the beginning. I can't even comprehend this.

I just ask my God daily, "Lord, put me in the place to receive your love most fully today." I've come to see that if I'm full of his love, it must flow out to those around me. I just cannot keep it in.

So, I listen, smile, love people with a hug or with my eyes. I share my story of surrender to his lordship and my experience of his love.

Yes, I have literature available in my car and home. I study the issues and strive to speak intelligently about pregnancy, abortion, and related issues. But Sis, regardless of what I know or don't know, I'm his ambassador—his representative to my little world. My responsibility is to show through my life that Jesus is alive, that he wants to love people and show them why they were created.

What a holy and awesome privilege to have access to other hurting, broken people and to connect them with the healer. Sometimes I'm not able to openly mention God's name to a client. But I pray they will come to feel worthwhile and to see "My Father's Eyes" in me.

Someone once wrote,

> You are writing each day a letter to all.
> Take care that the writing is true;
> For the only gospel that some may read
> Is the gospel according to you.

That says it all, doesn't it?

Sis, pray for me. I want Jesus to use me to love his own people back to him. I want to be his ambassador.

Thanks for listening.

26

Rest and Balance

Dear Sis,

I want to calm your fears that I'm headed for a breakdown. I'm really not. But I can understand your concern, looking on from a distance at the intense nature of my work at the pregnancy center. Believe me, I've seen this kind of work take its toll on people. If I ever lose my zest for celebration, laughter, and joy—please stop me!

I have always felt my life's work must have meaning on this earth and hereafter, so the jobs I have taken on over the years have tended to be stressful. Take all those years of teaching and counseling high school students for instance. Sometimes it seemed I would labor and labor without seeing much fruit at the time. But God would always give me enough encouragement to keep on: "Hang in there, you're planting special seeds of love; harvest time comes later."

I must admit, however, that I overworked myself in those years of masses of students and constant deadlines. I loved the work. But I had to learn the hard way—by getting sick—that I needed to pace myself.

Now, again, I find myself at a job where I'm prone to overwork, to overcommitment—where the needs never end. It amazes me at times to see how many crises (other than clients' crises) occur at a crisis pregnancy center. For several months, my time was out of control; it was subject to Charles Hummel's concept in *Tyranny of the Urgent* (Downers Grove, IL.: InterVarsity Christian Fellowship, 1967) where the greatest danger in life is letting the urgent things crowd out the important matters. Time for prayer, family, Bible study, fellowship, and rest often become usurped by the urgent tasks of the day that keep us moving at a feverish pace. The important things rarely cry out for attention until they become urgent.

This work can have a sneaky effect on us if we don't watch out. I guess I should speak for myself. The stories I hear from clients are like soap operas—the same basic themes; just the names and faces change:

low self-esteem,

sad family life,

no father in the house,

jail, drugs, physical or sexual abuse,

parents who act like they don't care,

distorted relationships, abortion.

They're all people looking for love in many of the wrong places! As a Christian, I know about the great Lover, Jesus, and his gift of abundant life. I know he promised we could experience that life here and hereafter. Yet most of our clients reveal fear, brokenness, rejections, pain, and isolation.

A steady diet of the seamy side of life can distort a person's view of reality. Is everyone this messed up?

I read recently that policemen who work in the ghetto districts often get sucked into the lifestyle of those they are sent to watch out for. Their heart goes out to prostitutes, for instance, and it's not uncommon for a cop to marry one! Or they spend so much time around drug users that they end up on drugs themselves.

I guess that's the danger of being exposed so often to a painful side of life—it starts to look normal. I know without the gift of perspective from you and others I couldn't keep on doing what I do.

I started this letter to assure you I'm not going to burn out. Over the years I've learned more about how to protect myself from going under. For instance, a booklet by Watchman Nee titled, *Ministry to the Lord or Ministry to the House,* (Los Angeles: Stream Publishers, n.d.) has constantly reminded me that my "first love" must always be Jesus—not getting caught up in ministry, doing good things. Quality personal time with my Maker is a basic necessity—more important, even, than feeding my physical body.

My patient and loving God doesn't pound me over the head when I neglect our prime time together. Yet, how stupid I am when I think I can accomplish anything on my own. It's so important for me to ask his guidance daily—to listen for his plan for the day. What would I do without my mainstay of his Word, my daily bread?

I do need regular breaks from this work. Restful sleep and a quiet place with no phones or people are a must for me to pursue seeking my Lord and enjoying His love for me. You'll notice I've been better at scheduling times away this past year. I usually opt to surround myself with *life*—spectacular beauty in nature, very special friends that I can just be me with, and families with kids who honestly love one another. I have a hunger to be with normal families interacting normally with each other, their God, and their world.

So Sis, don't worry, I'm getting better at "ordering my private world" to quote Gordon MacDonald who wrote a book about that (Chicago: Moody Press, 1984).

Even taking the time to write these letters is healing for my soul. Being quiet, thinking and feeling through a pen, sorting out my myriad of experiences as I walk with Jesus in this holy place—all these things bring healing to my whole being.

Lord, thank you for your words: "Come to me, all who labor and are heavy laden, and I will give you rest. Take my yoke upon you, and learn from me; for I am gentle and lowly in heart. . . . My yoke is easy, and my burden is light" (Matt. 11:28–30 RSV).

Lord, thanks for having big shoulders.

Sis, thanks again for listening.

27

Holidays

Dear Sis,
Christmas is fast approaching. There is so much going on at holiday time, but I must take time out to write this letter. I want to introduce you to:

Sandra	Victoria	Kathleen	Kristen
Stephanie	Sara Lee	Robert	Desiree
Allen	George	Samuel	Peter
Joseph	Andrew	Timothy	Jason
Garrett	Erica	Tammy	Ryan

These little ones will all celebrate their first Christmas this month. Their moms came through our pregnancy center this year and made the decision to bring them into the world. As we think of Jesus' arrival in Bethlehem, we pray that this Christmas will be a wonderful time for these cute and cuddly ones and their families.

These few names could easily represent three or more times as many children who were spared abortion this year through the help of our center—I certainly hope so! Often we are unable to follow up on the young women who come to our clinic for the free pregnancy test. Some

118

women do not want to be contacted. Others move or give false names or phone numbers. And so we won't know the true outcome till we reach heaven someday.

Christmas is a time of gift giving. The mothers of the babies named here chose to give themselves and their preborn children the gift of life. This year, when under extreme pressure to have an abortion (the so-called "easy way out"), these moms accepted the grace to choose life.

When I hear that phrase, "easy way out," I'm reminded of the prevailing lie about abortion. Abortion is *not* a "quick fix" to the crisis of an unwanted pregnancy. Many times a vulnerable woman is exploited into believing that abortion will give her back her freedom, her life. But a woman who aborts her child *loses* more life physically, emotionally, and spiritually than any of us can imagine.

As Mother Teresa so aptly says, "When a woman has an abortion there are two deaths—the baby in her womb and the spirit of the mother." The trauma women, men, and families suffer after abortions is real. Someday soon we will have the statistical data to prove it conclusively.

Sis, I started this letter talking about holidays and beautiful, bouncing babies, yet I have again been drawn to write about the trauma that women experience in abortion. The women and men who suffer after abortion and get help are the fortunate ones. Postabortion counseling—having someone to listen to the story and give permission to grieve, mourn, and name the baby that has been lost—is an important aspect of the healing process.

Pastor Thomas Klasen has written "A Pro-Life Manifesto" promoting a National Memorial to the Unborn for Washington, D.C., and mourning centers spread throughout the country. He believes firmly that as a society we need to name and recognize those children who were aborted. Just as we have a Vietnam Memorial he is recommending places where mourning is encouraged. Sis, I think he has an important point.

My most exciting Christmases have been those I celebrated since I started to work at the pregnancy center.

Repeatedly teaching the facts on fetal development, I am still overwhelmed with the picture of a half-billion tiny sperm headed for one ripe egg. One sperm penetrates the egg and presto, conception has occurred. Add nourishment, nine months of growing, and—wonder of wonders, miracle of miracles!

Our God decided to be even more spectacular with his Son's arrival on Christmas morn. Even though his people repeatedly said no to God's ways, he promised them a Savior. For centuries the Lord's chosen people waited for a Jewish messiah to deliver them. Then, at the perfect time in history, after centuries of specific prophecies, an angel declared to a young Jewish virgin, "Hail, O favored one . . ." (Luke 1:28 RSV).

Can't you sense the drama as all of heaven waited for God's Son to emerge from Mary's body. Angels and babies, no intercourse or husband—what a crisis pregnancy for Mary!

The experiences of Mary and Joseph, Mary and Elizabeth, the trip to Bethlehem and "no room in the inn" added to the suspense. Angels for the shepherds, stars for the wise men—all of creation strained to welcome the baby Jesus.

I'm sure Jesus looked like anybody who emerges from the womb. Yet this was the Father's only Son, his precious Jesus who put aside his kingship in heaven to come to this planet earth, wear diapers (or their equivalent); be hungry, wet, cold, and messy. Why would Jesus come and take on our flesh? The Father had to show us how much we meant to him, so he sent his very best—his own Son—to love us in a way history had never seen.

The sense of drama, adventure and wonder is awesome. How much our God must care—that he would send a little baby to tell us he wants to be in relationship with us.

Sis, the Christmas carol "What Child Is This?" will always search my heart at holiday time.

What child is this, who laid to rest,
On Mary's lap is sleeping?
Whom angels greet with anthems sweet,
While shepherds watch are keeping?

This, this is Christ the King,
Whom shepherds guard and angels sing:
Haste, haste to bring him laud,
The babe, the Son of Mary.

William C. Dix, 1837–1898

Thanks for listening. Let's make this the best Jesus-filled Christmas yet!

28

Cracked Pots

Dear Sis,

Every day at the pregnancy center brings totally different kinds of people. It may be our location, our advertising, our word-of-mouth reputation, or the fact that we pray for every client who comes through the doors or calls on the phones. The interaction between clients and volunteers or staff at the center has one very prominent characteristic. At our center, people share their pain with strangers.

This work is unique. Though every human being walking the face of the earth has problems, hardships, and struggles, most people work hard to show that "I can handle it" or "I've got it together." What brings most women and men to the pregnancy center is their crisis of a possible unwanted pregnancy with its intense and overwhelming life decisions.

I think of the seventeen-year-old popular Catholic teen who was taking a prescribed medication with strong warnings on the label—the pharmaceutical company clearly encouraged abortion if a woman became pregnant while on the medicine. And the student believed she was carrying a six-week-old preborn child inside her womb. In class she had often argued against abortion with her peers. How she cried! In between sobs she would say, "I must abort; I can't carry this child." She felt she couldn't talk to her Christian parents saying, "They'll be so disappointed in me, the embarrassment will be too great, they'll make us break up." How sad it was to watch the one point in her life when she needed the love, input, and support of her parents yet she wouldn't talk to them.

She did choose abortion, and a couple years later reappeared at the center. At nineteen she was no longer "an irresponsible teen," as she called herself. She had come back to say, "You were right. I knew it was a baby— my baby girl. I thought I could talk myself into believing I had to abort because of the medicine. The guilt, shame, and remorse paralyzed me. I had to get right with God and the church, and I had to forgive myself. I can't change my decision. I'm really sorry for what I've done. I know I still need a lot of healing, but I'm on my way. In fact, I've helped several friends in college who've had abortions and a couple who were headed that way. I shared my story, and they listened. They each said that what I shared made a great impression on them. I could see in their eyes that they knew I cared and identified with their pain."

Sis, a story like this doesn't happen very often. It usually takes many years of denial and often bizarre behavior before a woman begins to face and work through the abortion experience. What a victory to see such growth! But, oh, the cost! The pain is so real.

The other story that comes to mind is another Catholic woman who recently came to our clinic for a pregnancy test and ended up staying for counseling. She wanted desperately to be pregnant; she and her husband had been trying for three years without success. But she had been pregnant once—four years earlier, when she was newly married. She had been excited about the baby—a little scared, but eager to start a family. Then, a few weeks into the pregnancy, she "didn't feel quite right."

When she developed right-sided pains in her abdomen, fever, and chills, she had called the doctor, who met her and her husband at the emergency room. An ectopic or tubal pregnancy had been diagnosed, and everybody had pushed Cynthia to have an abortion: "The tube and baby must come out, or you both will die." The doctor, family, and close friends had all added their input. The parish priest had said, "Yes, ectopic pregnancy is one of those life-or-death cases in which you need to do as the doctor says and remove that tube."

Now a steady stream of tears flowed as Cynthia shared her story with me. "I feel like I killed my baby—the guilt really gets to me at times. In fact, I think that's why I can't get pregnant. The priest, the doctor, my husband, and others—all say I shouldn't feel guilty, I did the best thing. But there are times I think I should have died too."

Cynthia had never been given permission to feel her loss. As a result, anxiety, fear, excitement, confusion, guilt, anger, grief, remorse were balled up together inside her. But as she sorted through the emotions in our counseling sessions, her whole posture seemed to change. As she retold the story, mourned and named the baby—Joseph Anthony—committed him to God, and forgave herself, dramatic improvements could be seen. It took her a couple sessions to work through the anger at the doctor, priest, and others who had pushed her. Cynthia's healing is still in process, and last visit she announced, "I actually have hope that my next pregnancy test will be positive."

Sis, these women are two examples of the "walking wounded" among us. Some would use the expression "cracked pots." I imagine a little ceramic potpourri pot with holes all around, a candle inside, and sweet-scented herbs on top. Without those holes there would be no light seen, no fragrance enjoyed. The holes are our wounds, our wonderful cracks that allow God's light to shine out to the world and the aroma of his love to fill the air around us.

The volunteers and staff who work at our center are cracked pots, too—women and men with wounds and scars who freely share their pain with strangers in our center. To minister to the walking wounded, we must first be in touch with our own wounds and cracked places. When you know you're a "cracked pot," it's easier to provide an atmosphere where it's OK to share the hurts. Cracked pots when mended are stronger than when new. Lord, in our weakness make us strong. God, thanks for being so gentle in loving us to life and healing.

Sis, thanks for listening.

29

The Father's Heart

Dear Sis,

On All Saints Day, November 1, I attended the funeral of a dear old friend, a woman in her eighties. She had been a member of our prayer group—a beautiful example to us "younguns" of what it means to live with Jesus every step of every day.

Mary left behind five children, twenty-nine grand-children, and thirty-three great-grandchildren. As I sat behind all those family members at the service, my tears wouldn't stop. I was sorry to have lost Mary, yet happy to celebrate the day of her "graduation" to be with her Jesus. I was sad for the family who no longer had their saint among them.

But my tears went deeper than my sorrow for Mary or my compassion for her family. In fact, it took about twenty-four hours for me to pinpoint the reason for the heaviness and many, many tears.

Sis, when I saw the result of Mary's fruitfulness—the wonderful family she left behind, I couldn't help but remember the babies who never had a chance! I know the big statistics; these numbers are too staggering for my mind to comprehend. So instead I started thinking about the clients I had seen at our pregnancy center—those who went on to choose abortion for the children in their wombs.

Sis, you've heard me say many times that those of us working in crisis pregnancy centers can't be there just to save babies—that we must first be able to love women in crisis. With all I'm studying these days about postabortion trauma, I could go on and on about the hurts of these pregnant women, the second victims of abortion. But today I'm tuned into those babies.

Each baby that existed a few days or weeks after conception was made in the image of our God. That preborn child gives glory to God by being what it's called to be—a growing little person learning to be loved and responding to that love. How wonderful that our God would trust us with showing his love and care to this world!

Sis, you know that a lot of attention has focused on Bernard Nathanson's film, *Silent Scream*. Its title comes from the ultrasound pictures that show a preborn child during an abortion opening its mouth as if to scream. The extent of anguish and torture such a child experiences is known to God alone.

Our God hears that silent scream. My Father in heaven knows the excruciating pain of watching his only Son, Jesus, die violently. The agony in the garden of Gethsemane, the scourging at the pillar, the crowning with thorns, the carrying of the cross, the isolation and abandonment by friends, and finally the last breath—all were known intimately by his Father.

Sis, I believe that Christ's heart is filled with compassion and anguish when a child is aborted.

Lord, replace our stony hearts with your heart.

Thanks for listening, Sis.

30

Singleness

Dear Sis,

When I attend conferences for directors of crisis pregnancy centers I am always struck with the number of beautiful, intelligent, enthusiastic, and godly single women in their late twenties and thirties. It's as if God has handpicked an army of talented, dedicated women leaders who love Jesus and called them to devote some of the best years of their lives to running pregnancy centers.

Don't get me wrong. In this work there are also married women with children, a few men, some separated or divorced people, some widows and widowers, some single parents. I guess being single myself, I naturally notice my sisters in Christ who have enlisted in the same army as I have and are fighting battles in their part of the kingdom.

Sis, remember that during my first month of directing our center, I attended a talk by the director of a West Coast crisis pregnancy center—a vivacious thirty-nine-year-old woman of God? She said with absolute conviction, "God has equipped me with education, experience, and a desire to serve him in this pro-life work. I will probably never be as free to devote time and energy to the pregnancy center as I am right now. God knows what he is doing, and I trust him. Singleness is his best for me at this moment of my journey. I have never been as happy and fulfilled. The desire he's given me for marriage and a family is in his hands. Meanwhile, I'm working for Jesus and seeking him first."

Sis, I will never forget the sparkle in that woman's eyes and the power in her words. What an example—and what a wonderful role model for me, a brand-new, single, pregnancy-center director.

But being unmarried is not the only kind of singleness. Another kind comes to mind—the kind of singlemindedness that can end up making an idol of pro-life work. As in many other areas in life, eating, work, drugs, church, spending, and pleasure—we can so easily get off balance.

Sis, with our tendency toward extremes, what will keep us on track? Yet another form of singleness—a singlehearted attitude toward seeking God. I keep my balance by asking Jesus to be first in every area of my life—asking him to help me with my priorities, goals, and use of time. I guess the same thing was said centuries ago in the two great commandments: "Love God with your whole heart, mind, soul, and strength" and "Love your neighbor as yourself" (Luke 10:27, paraphrased). That's easy to quote, but living it out takes a lifetime!

It amazes me that God chooses to need us—that he needs our hands, feet, eyes, and hearts to reach out to others with his unconditional love. In the counseling room at the pregnancy center, Jesus-in-me listens and loves the Jesus-in-need that I meet in the client across from me. Sometimes his presence becomes so real in the counseling room that I want to take off my shoes, sensing I'm on holy ground.

Sis, I want to end this letter with yet another prayer. Our Father in heaven, from whom every family gets its name, be with us now. Place in our hearts your holy desire to see your kingdom of peace and love established here in our midst. We want to put you first, Lord.

For those of us you have called to a single state of life now, help us to be singlehearted toward you. Enable us to live lives pleasing to you alone. Give us your vision as to how you want to use the gifts and talents you have given us. Unfold a bit more of your plan regarding the pro-life work you've placed before us. Show us keys to stopping the holocaust, to preventing the desire for wrong relationships, to healing the brokenhearted. Make our lives count, Lord.

For those of us with a desire for spouses and children, we give those hopes and dreams to you and trust your perfect timing. We seek our fulfillment in loving you and making you loved by the hurting world around us. Thank you for the precious gift of life. Jesus, a special thanks for being the Way, the Truth, and the Life! And God—Daddy—thank you for hearing the prayer of our hearts even before we ask.

Sis, thanks for listening.

31

Hope

Dear Sis,

This work at the center is often a juggling act. One minute I am speaking to teens about abortion, post-abortion stress, or saying no to premarital sex. Next I am training volunteers in counseling skills or doing pregnancy tests. And then I'm meeting with a pregnant teen and her parents who want to talk about options; or fund-raising for special projects such as cribs, maternity care, or housing for homeless single moms with children. The needs never disappear—at times it feels like I'm trying to sweep back the ocean with a broom.

Then I look at the facts about abortion that I often quiz students on to see what they know. (Most times when I speak I find that people don't have a basic knowledge of the facts of abortion.) I've mentioned them to you before:

Four thousand four hundred babies a day are aborted in the United States, or one every eighteen seconds.

Fifty-five million are aborted a year worldwide.

One percent (40 per day) of all abortions occur beyond the twenty-first week of pregnancy.

In many states minors can have abortions without parental knowledge or approval.

It's legal to abort up through all nine months of pregnancy because *Roe vs. Wade* decision stated we don't know when personhood begins.

It's a five-hundred million dollar a year industry in the United States.

Fathers have no legal right to prevent their children from being aborted.

Problems, problems, problems. A guaranteed way to become unable to function in this job is to stay focused on the problems, the heartbreaks, the mounting needs, the ocean that wants to wash me away.

Sis, I've mentioned rest, balance, family, laughter, priorities, prayer, and a good support system as ingredients for survival in pregnancy center work. There's also an elusive quality that you can't manufacture, but you know when you have it and when you don't. It's *hope.*

Focusing on the problems will make me hopeless. But what brings me hope?

Sis,—it's the stories! It's remembering individual clients who have called or walked through our doors and the ways God has arranged "divine appointments." I think of the client whom we asked, "How did you hear about us?" She answered, "Directory assistance. I called information to get the phone number and address of an abortion clinic, and they gave me this pregnancy center." Sis, she came without calling us and walked in expecting an abortion clinic. When she found out we don't do abortions, she started crying with relief, because she really didn't want the abortion but needed help and support to carry her baby. What a wonderful God-incidence!

I remember the married woman who had two kids, one miscarriage, and one baby stillborn when it was almost full-term. She was grieving so badly while everyone around her told her she should "be over it by now." Helping her and her husband work through their sorrow and unresolved feelings and be at peace with their "two angels" in heaven was quite an experience. Shortly after she finished counseling she arrived for a pregnancy test—positive—and nine months later gave birth to a ten-pound bouncing baby boy. Thanks, Lord!

I think of the Christmas season, when lots of anonymous gifts and packages arrive at the center for the clients and their babies. What a privilege to be channels of generosity to those in need!

I also remember the sixteen-year-old black student from an alcoholic family whose pregnancy test was negative. After a long discussion about her life, she told me, "I'm making adult decisions, being involved in these sexual relationships, but I'm not ready to take on the consequences. I can't stop myself. Help me stay on the right track. I don't want to keep making wrong choices." Wow—a life had been touched!

Sis, you know I can go on forever with stories of the big things and little ones too that I see God doing every day. Hope means being open for God's surprises—and his work is full of surprises.

I need to close with a prayer:

Dear Daddy in heaven, you are the only one to give me hope this day. Thanks for the growth in the number of crisis pregnancy centers, rescue operations, and postabortion counseling ministries. Thanks for the action in the courts and on Capitol Hill. Thanks for the chances you give me to be stretched and challenged to love in brand-new ways at the center.

Lord Jesus, your death on the cross was really a victory. That is such a mystery. Thanks for being the God who brings life out of death, joy in the midst of suffering, and hope in place of despair. Keep me dependent on you for everything and aware that you have called me to love—one person at a time.

And thanks for listening.

A Note
to the Reader

Now that you have finished this book, I hope these letters have captured your heart. Any crisis pregnancy center director or experienced volunteer could recount similar stories of the joys and heartaches of this ministry.

In your neighborhood there are volunteers at your local crisis pregnancy center, wonderfully compassionate giving saints who make substantial sacrifices of their time, money, and energies to be available to those in crisis. My pastor would say "compassion" is "helping one's heart around the corner." The need for more centers, more volunteers and supporters grows daily. Will you help another's heart around the corner?

Bill Bair, author of *Love Is an Open Door* (New York: Steward Press, 1974) recently challenged me during a banquet speech. He asked, "If you had all the power in the world what would you do with it?" He repeated the question again, directing us to consider our answer. "If I had all the power in the world would I stop abortion, disease, suffering, war, the desire for evil? What would I do?"

Bill's answer was, "Jesus had all the power in the world and he washed feet." Again, I was convinced of the truth of gently, lovingly, caring for each person Jesus sends just as he has so lavishly loved me.

The crisis pregnancy center closest to you could probably give you a list of at least ten ways you could be a footwasher, meeting needs of your neighbors in crisis. Will you consider answering the call to become part of the solution? Resources of books, programs, and services are listed on the subsequent pages. Please pray and listen for God's answer. Obeying his call will challenge you to grow and the rewards are great. Talk to your local volunteers about how and why they answered the call. Discover for yourself why they were "caring enough to help."

I'd like to end with two special quotes:

Let there be no misunderstanding. The fight for life and truth is not for professional warriors, but for those common folk who love peace. We simply want to get back to the business of living decent lives, knowing that the weak and defenseless among us are cared for and respected. We do not enjoy resistance, but we will endure it in the interest of Truth. We just believe that children should be born . . . all children. Is that so radical?

Jeff Ostrander in *From the Field*, Linda E. Perry and Cyndi Philkill, eds., Greater Baltimore Crisis Pregnancy Center, Inc., 1989, (Baltimore, MD: p. 49).

People were also bringing babies to Jesus to have him touch them. When the disciples saw this, they rebuked them. But Jesus called the children to him and said, "Let the little children come to me, and do not hinder them, for the Kingdom of God belongs to such as these. I tell you the truth, any one who will not receive the Kingdom of God like a child will never enter it." Luke 18:15–17 (NIV)

Thank you very much for listening.

Shalom,

Ellen Curro

Suggested Resources for Further Reading and Groups that Provide Services

Crisis Pregnancy Services

Auburne Center
7701 Belair Rd.
Baltimore, MD 21236
800-492-5530

Bethany Christian Services
901 Eastern, NE
Grand Rapids, MI 49503
800-BETHANY

Birthright International
686 N. Broad Street
Woodbury, NJ 08096
800-848-LOVE

Liberty Godparent Foundation
P.O. Box 27000
Lynchburg, VA 24506
800-542-4453

Christian Action Council
701 W. Broad Street, #405
Falls Church, VA 22046
703-237-2100

Pearson Foundation
3663 Lindell Boulevard, Suite 290
St. Louis, MO 63108
800-633-2252, Ext. 700

Books on Crisis Pregnancies

Dacy, Matthew, Dacy, Lea, and Jackson, Dave, *Teen Pregnancy*. Elgin, IL: David C. Cook Publishing, 1989.

Hudson, Jane, and Hudson, Amy, *Season of Shadow*. Cincinnati: Standard Publishing Co., 1989.

Johnson, Lissa Halls, *Just Like Ice Cream*. Palm Springs, CA: Ronald N. Haynes Publishers, 1982.

O'Brien, Beverly, *Mom . . . I'm Pregnant*. Wheaton, IL: Tyndale House Publishers, 1982.

Perry, Linda E., and Philkill, Cyndi, eds., *From the Field*. Baltimore, MD: Greater Baltimore Crisis Pregnancy Center, 1989.

Pierson, Anne, *My Baby and Me*. Lancaster, PA: Loving and Caring, 1984.

Roggow, Linda, and Owen, Carolyn, *Handbook for Pregnant Teens*. Grands Rapids, MI: Zondervan, 1984.

Zimmerman, Martha, *Should I Keep My Baby?* Minneapolis, MN: Bethany House Publishers, 1983.

Books on Life Before Birth

Caretto, Carlo, *Journey Without End*. Notre Dame, IN: Ave Maria Press, 1989.

Garton, Jean Staker, *Who Broke The Baby?* Minneapolis, MN: Bethany Fellowship, Inc. 1979.

Hanes, Mari, *The Child Within*. Wheaton, IL: Living Books, 1983.

MacNutt, Francis, and MacNutt, Judith, *Praying for Your Unborn Child*. New York: Doubleday, 1988.

Nilsson, Lennart, *A Child Is Born*. New York: Delacorte Press, 1977.

Shettles, Landrum, and Rorvik, David, *Rites of Life*. Grand Rapids, MI: Zondervan, 1983.

Verny, Thomas, and Kelly, John, *Secret Life of the Unborn Child*. New York: Summit Books, 1981 (Note: pro-choice position).

Programs on Abstinence (for teens)

Adolescent Family Life Program OPA/OAPP
200 Independence Avenue, S.W.
HHH Building, Room 736E
Washington, DC 20201

American Life League
P.O. Box 1350
Stafford, VA 22554

Couple to Couple League
P.O. Box 11084
Cincinnati, OH 45211

Eagle Forum
P.O. Box 618
Alton, IL 62002

Focus on the Family
801 Corporate Center Drive
Pomona, CA 91764

The Foundation for the Family
P.O. Box 389155
Cincinnati, OH 45238

Human Life Center
University of Steubenville
Steubenville, OH 43952

Human Life International
7845-E Airpark Road
Gaithersburg, MD 20879

Last Days Ministries
P.O. Box 40
Lindale, TX 75711-0040

Living World Publications Office
2606 1/2 W. 8th Street
Los Angeles, CA 90057

Sex Respect
P.O. Box 349
Bradley, IL 60915

Search Institute
122 W. Franklin Avenue, Suite 215
Minneapolis, MN 55404

TEEN AID
North 1330 Calispel
Spokane, WA 99201

Teen Star
8514 Bradmorc Drive
Bethesda, MD 20817

Why Wait?
P.O. Box 1000
Dallas, TX 75221

Womanity
1700 Oak Park Boulevard, C-4
Pleasant Hill, CA 94523

Resources on Adoption

Bethany Christian Services
901 Eastern, N.E.
Grand Rapids, MI 49503
800-BETHANY

Catholic Charities USA
1319 F. Street, NW
Washington, DC 20004
202-639-8400

National Committee on Adoption
1930 17th Street, NW
Washington, DC 20009
202-328-1200

Books on Adoption

Anderson, Anne Kiemel, *And With the Gift Came Laughter.* Wheaton, IL: Tyndale House Publishers, 1987.

Donnelly, Douglas R., *A Guide to Adoption.* Pomona, CA: Focus on the Family, 1988.

National Committee on Adoption, *The Adoption Fact Book.* Washington, D.C.: National Committee on Adoption, 1989.

Project Share, *The Adoption Option: A Guidebook for Pregnancy Counselors.* Rockville, MD: Project Share, 1986.

Sandford, Paula, *New Life For Your Adopted Child.* Coeur d'Alene, ID: Elijah House, 1982.

Waters, Ethel, *His Eye Is on the Sparrow.* New York: Doubleday & Co., 1950.

Books on Abortion Information

Andrusko, Dave, ed., *To Rescue the Future.* Toronto: Life Cycle Books, 1983.

Burtchaell, James T., *Rachel Weeping.* Kansas City: Andrews and McMeel, 1982.

Ficarra, Bernard T., *Abortion Analyzed.* Old Town, Maine: Health Educator Publications, 1989.

Grant, George, *Grand Illusions.* Brentwood, TN: Wolgemuth and Hyatt Publishers, 1989.

Nathanson, Bernard, and Ostling, Richard, *Aborting America.* New York: Doubleday, 1979.

Powell, John, *Abortion: The Silent Holocaust.* Allen, TX: Argus, 1981.

Saltenberg, Ann, *Every Woman Has a Right to Know the Dangers of Legal Abortion.* Glassboro, NJ: Air-Plus Enterprises, 1983.

Van Winden, Lori, *The Case Against Abortion*. Ligouri, MO: Ligouri Publications, 1988.

Wilke, John and Wilke, Barbara, *Abortion, Questions & Answers*. Cincinnati: Hayes Publishing, 1988.

Wilke, John, *Handbook on Abortion*. Cincinnati: Hayes Publishing, 1979.

Young, Curtis J., *The Least of These*. Chicago: Moody Press, 1983.

Books on Healing After an Abortion, Miscarriage or Stillbirth

Baker, Don, *Beyond Choice: The Abortion Story No One Is Telling*. Portland, OR: Multnomah Press, 1985.

Cochrane, Linda, *Women in Ramah: A Postabortion Bible Study*. Falls Church, VA: Christian Action Council Education and Ministries Fund, 1987.

Ervin, Paula, *Women Exploited: The Other Victims of Abortion*. Huntington, IN: Our Sunday Visitor, 1985.

Hayford, Jack, *Early Flight*. Van Nuys, CA: Living Ways Ministries, 1986.

Klasen, Thomas G., *A Pro-Life Manifesto*. Westchester, IL: Crossway Books, 1988.

Koerbel, Pam, *Abortion's Second Victim*. Wheaton, IL: Victor Books, 1986.

Kuenning, Delores, *Helping People Through Grief*. Minneapolis, MN: Bethany House Publishers, 1987.

Linn, Dennis, Linn, Matthew, and Fabricant, Sheila, *Healing the Greatest Hurt*. Mahwah, NJ: Paulist Press, 1985.

Mannion, Michael T., *Abortion and Healing: A Cry to be Whole*. Kansas City, MO: Sheed and Ward, 1986.

Michels, Nancy, *Helping Women Recover from Abortion*. Minneapolis, MN: Bethany House Publishers, 1988.

Peretti, Frank E., *Tilly*. Westchester, IL: Crossway Books, 1988.

Rank, Maureen, *Free to Grieve*. Minneapolis, MN: Bethany House Publishers, 1985.

Reisser, Teri, and Reisser, Paul, *Help for the Postabortion Woman*. Grand Rapids, MI: Zondervan Publishing House, 1989.

Reardon, David D., *Aborted Women: Silent No More*. Westchester, IL: Crossway Books, 1987.

Rye, Nancy, *Handling the Heartbreak of Miscarriage*. San Bernadino, CA: Here's Life Publishers, 1987.

Schostak, Arthur, and McClouth, Gary, *Men and Abortion*. New York: Praeger Publishers, 1984 (Note: strong pro-choice position).

Seamands, David A., *Healing for Damaged Emotions*. Wheaton, IL: Victor Books, 1981.

Speckhard, Anne, *Postabortion Counseling: A Manual for Christian Counselors*. Falls Church, VA: PACE, Christian Action Council, 1987.

Stanford, Susan, *Will I Cry Tomorrow?* Old Tappan, NJ: Fleming Revell, 1987.

Vredevelt, Pam W., *Empty Arms*. Portland, OR: Multnomah Press, 1984.

Postabortion Support and Materials

Abortion Trauma Services and Outreach
1608 13th Avenue S., #11R
Birmingham, AL 35202
205-939-0302

American Victims of Abortion
Olivia Gans, Director
419 7th Street, NW, Suite 402
Washington, DC 20004
202-626-8800

Association for Interdisciplinary Research in Values and
Social Change
Wanda Franz, Ph.D., President
419 7th Street, NW, Suite 500
Washington, DC 20004
202-626-8800

Heart Light
P.O. Box 8513
Green Bay, WI 54308
414-468-8444

National Office of Post-Abortion Reconciliation and
Healing, Inc.
Vicki Thorn
St. John's Center
3680 S. Kinnickinnic Avenue
Milwaukee, WI 53207
414-447-7386

Open ARMS (Abortion-Related Ministries)
National Headquarters
6919 E. 10th Street, F-10
Indianapolis, IN 46219
317-359-9950

PACE Post-Abortion Counseling & Education
Christian Action Council
701 W. Broad Street, #405
Falls Church, VA 22046
703-237-2100

Victim of Choice
Nola Jones, Director
124 Shefield Drive
Vacaville, CA 95688
707-448-6015

WEBA Women Exploited by Abortion
24823 Nogal Street
Morena Valley, CA 92388
714-247-1278

Books on Nonviolent Direct Action

Giudo, Richard Cowden, ed., *If You Reject Them, You Reject Me, The Prison Letters of Joan Andrews*. Manassas, VA: Trinity Communication, 1989.

Scheidler, Joseph M., *Closed: 99 Ways to Stop Abortion*. Lake Bluff, IL: Regnery Books, 1985.

Terry, Randall, *Operation Rescue*. Springdale, PA: Whitaker House Publishing, 1989.